8 Billy Wilder

Billy Wilder

Axel Madsen

Indiana University Press
Bloomington and London

subj. o.k.

The Cinema One series is published by
Indiana University Press
in association with Sight and Sound
and the Education Department of the
British Film Institute

First United States Publication 1969

Library of Congress catalog card number: 68–66392

Printed in Great Britain

Contents

Cover: Billy Wilder

1: Portrait

'You're Norma Desmond. You used to be in pictures.
You used to be big.'
'I *am* big. It's the pictures that got small.'
Sunset Boulevard

Billy Wilder is a compact man scowling at the world through glasses and perennial cigarette smoke. He was shooting the wedding scene of *Irma la Douce* when I met him the first time.

The Goldwyn Studio set is bustling with extras dressed up as a cross-section of Rue Saint-Denis humanity, including *flics* and *boueux*—without brooms but with the Ville de Paris coat of arms on their caps. All speak soft Californian. On the adjoining stage, Alex Trauner's re-creation of a fictitious Les Halles street, Rue Casanova, stands empty this afternoon, and to walk through this silent re-created Paris—*the* 'in' attraction in Hollywood during the winter of 1962–63—is hallucinating. Steadfast Trauner has outdone himself, the columnists are cooing. Authenticity is Wilder's first commandment of make-believe.

But the action this late afternoon is in the sawed-off Notre-Dame. Wilder looks tired, sitting on top of a step-ladder, his favourite set-side seat, in a lonely corner of the stage while Joseph LaShelle and his assistants are lighting the church décor. The extras are clustered in groups, some playing cards on an upturned soft-drink case, and the assistant is already handing out the next day's call-sheet. Jack Lemmon is chain-smoking while a wardrobe girl stitches a shoulder of his Nestor Marriage tuxedo No. 1. Shirley MacLaine is resting in her trailer. Several extras gaze at their watches, wondering—if not hoping—that the scene will go into overtime.

7

Wilder on the Rue Casanova set: *Irma la Douce*

Tom Ewell, Wilder, Marilyn Monroe and subway grating: *The Seven Year Itch*

'Yes, we're the old wave,' yawns Wilder in French, climbing down from his ladder. 'De la moyenne vague tirant sur la vieille.' His brown eyes twinkle behind the glasses and he smiles at his own pun, happy still to be able to coin phrases in his melodious if somewhat rusty Viennese French. 'My pictures are not intended to reform people; hopefully they are stories sufficiently intriguing to make them forget the popcorn.'

LaShelle is ready and floods the flat-topped Notre-Dame with 20,000 watts, suddenly giving shadow and relief to the stucco pillars and painted-on sandstone walls. Wilder crosses to the camera while assistants herd the extras into the pews and someone is sent to fetch 'Irma MacLaine'. Wilder swings into the camera seat and, through the viewfinder, 'blocks' his church crowd. He makes a husky butcher stand up in one row, a lady with a hat sit down, and has the standing background close in behind the pews. The plot-line has Inspector Lefevre (Herschel Bernardi) rushing into the church followed by two uniformed policemen—evidently seconds too late to stop the marriage, which once summarily per- formed, has Irma fainting in labour pains and Nestor carrying her to the vestry where a healthy baby is born with the fade-out.

Wilder rehearses once with bowler-hatted Bernardi shouldering his way through the standing background and freezing as he sees the ceremony. To focus the extras' apparently wandering eyes, Wilder has a baby spot set up on the altar just out of camera range and orders his Parisians to concentrate their collective gaze on it. The priest comes in, followed by nine-month pregnant Irma in flowing bridal gown.

The rest goes quickly and painlessly. The bell silences the set, and on the assistant's 'Roll 'em!', the priest takes up his back-to-camera position. At the soundman's muffled 'Speed!', Irma and Nestor kneel in the foreground; at 'Rolling!', Lemmon squashes out his cigarette and finds his proper facial expression; and at Wilder's soft 'Action!', Inspector Lefevre starts to push himself through the background. He freezes and takes off his hat . . . slowly. 'Cut!'

One take. One only.

Wilder's set-side antics, sarcasm, bullying and cajoling are legendary, and tongues as sharp as his own have said that seeing Wilder directing is often more entertaining than seeing a Wilder film.

Wilder is an unending flow of talk and he gets his performances out of his actors with insults, puns and snappy jokes. As all legends, however, his clowning is often an exaggeration by journalists looking for crisp copy. Wilder on the *Irma la Douce* set that day was a model of economy of gestures and efficiency. Wilder's life *is* a model of dignified affluence—unostentatious reserve and caustic resilience.

For a man whose films have grossed at an estimated $80 million, the bubbling and balding misanthrope lives in spartan splendour. Wilder and his wife, Audrey, are considered the social leaders for a large chunk of the movie world's élite, yet they don't live on a landscaped spread of Beverly Hills real estate with kidney-shaped swimming-pool and built-in screening-room, but an apartment on Wilshire Boulevard. Wilder's Goldwyn Studio office is comfortable, but has nothing of a movie mogul's traditional megalomania. For

9

Wilder rehearses: *Irma la Douce* (*left, and top far right*) and *The Fortune Cookie* →

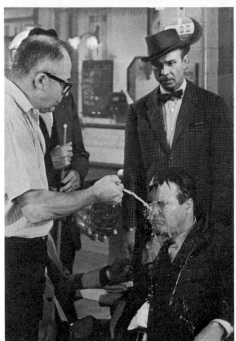

all his prominence, Wilder has no entourage, and many of his friends are linked only indirectly to the entertainment industry . . . if at all. Billy and Audrey are great go-outers, but their idea of entertaining at home is a lively game of bridge.

The Westwood Towers is a highrise in the elegant but not chic section of West Los Angeles, and the Wilder apartment on the 12th is cosy and comfortable. Originally, it was quite large for two people, but Wilder's constant art purchases have slowly crammed the rooms. The terrace sports Wilder's collection of Bonsai trees and the living-room is festooned with art. When he fled Berlin in 1933, he had rolled-up canvases under his arm, and sarcastic friends say he collected art before he collected money. Besides the works by Klee, Kirchner and Jawlensky—which mirror his Central European roots—Vuillard, Picasso, de Stael, Chagall, Dufy and Rouault sprout from the walls, reflecting a lifelong love of things French. Shahn, Rivers, Cornell and Johnson demonstrate his Americanisation; Balthus, Schiele and Pascin his sophistication in erotica; and Bombois and Vivin his penchant for humour.

Wilder is an excellent bridge-player, and he is a member of a bridge set which meets every Saturday and Sunday and sometimes in between. The game is noisy with lots of jokes. 'Billy is a regular winner in that game and not because he's a great technician,' says Alfred Sheinwold, a professional player. 'He can't be bothered with that. He's a good technician, but more than anybody else, he plays the people. Bridge-players would use the expression: He always knows where the Queen of Spades is.' Wilder is an avid sports fan and a good chess-player, and loves to fly kites at his beach-house north of Malibu on windy days. He won't play chess any more, however, because it takes too long.

Indeed, restlessness is Wilder's most striking physical trait. Screenplays are written pacing the floor, and one of his habits when shooting is to go off into a corner and try out the things he will ask his actors to do in their next scene.

'Speed is absolutely of the essence to him,' says screenwriter Walter Reisch, who has known him since Vienna. 'He cannot do anything slowly. If he enters a party and everybody is talking slowly, he leaves. People who insist on finishing their sentences drive him crazy—he wants to write it himself. That's why he likes paintings—they don't talk back. That's his only fear in life . . . to be bored. He cannot stand to be with people who bore him . . . which doesn't mean he doesn't like them or respect them—he just doesn't mingle with them.'

Wilder is rarely in bed before 2 a.m., but he is in the office early, pacing the floor most of the day. His immense collection of canes, crops, shillelaghs, Indian war-clubs and even flint-edged axes, are in use during the pacing. Because he has back pains, he uses a cane to scratch or hit his back. 'The pains are not psycho-somatic,' he says if anyone brings this up, 'but the result of making love to girls in doorways in my youth, standing up.'

Audrey will smile and come forth with her own swipes on such occasions, making innuendoes about his masculine prowess today as a result of vertical coitus in his youthful years. Wilder met Audrey Young in 1944, during the shooting of *The Lost Weekend*. In it, she played a checkroom girl handing Ray Milland his hat as he was being thrown out of a bar. Wilder cut the scene so that only her forearm appeared, and both Wilders agreed that the forearm gave a superb performance. Wilder's first wife, from whom he is divorced, the daughter of a prominent lawyer, now lives in San Francisco with his only child, a daughter. Max Wilder, Billy's father, died in Berlin in 1926 and his mother remarried. Wilder never saw his family after he came to America as his mother, grandmother and stepfather died in concentration camps. 'My mother died around 1940, 1941—I could never find out exactly when—but I know through the Red Cross that she was gassed in Auschwitz.'

Toward the end of the Second World War, Wilder was appointed head of the U.S. Army's Psychological Warfare Division. He spent 1945 in Germany and, with the rank of Colonel, was over-seeing the programme content of all theatres and radio stations in the U.S. Zone. The nearest he got to action, wrote Richard Lemon in a feature article on Wilder,★ was a time when someone

★ *Saturday Evening Post*, 17 December 1966

requisitioned champagne and it exploded. Thinking they were under fire, Wilder led his men under their jeep.

'After the war, some Germans wanted to put on a passion play, and a carpenter wrote me asking permission to play Jesus. After we screened them, we found out that six of the Apostles were Gestapo men and the carpenter a stormtrooper. I said, "Yes, as long as the nails are real." '

Germany is a long story, and yet for an Austrian Jew whose family disappeared in the Nazi ovens Wilder bears remarkably little rancour or hatred. He was back in Berlin in 1947 shooting *A Foreign Affair*, a film that hit U.S. Army morale harder than the vanquished nation, and had Marlene Dietrich embodying all the worldly-wise sophistication of war-weary Germans, telling a Congresswoman what frumps American women are. In 1961, he shot *One, Two, Three* in Berlin, hiring Hubert von Meyerinck, Karl Ludwig Lindt and several other old friends. Wilder's total lack of banal sentimentality makes him coin gags about camps and Nazism. Otto Preminger is one of Wilder's friends, and although he is Jewish he resembles a Central Casting Nazi so much that Wilder had him play the Kommandant in *Stalag 17*. After the filming, when Preminger had left Hollywood on a trip and someone asked Wilder where he was, Wilder said, 'In his summer home—in Belsen.'

Wilder smokes four packs of cigarettes a day, and once remarked that he would give it up except that he might be hit by a car and he would hate to be lying there in the gutter bleeding to death and thinking about all the fun he had missed. Defining happiness, he said it is having a doctor who himself smokes four packs a day. Billy's remaining hair is cut in what he would probably call neo-Prussian crew cut, and his favourite attire is slacks and loose-hanging sweaters.

Wilder's malice is legendary. Among people struck by his meanness is George Axelrod, who wrote *The Seven Year Itch* as a play and then worked on the movie version with Wilder. When Axelrod reported to the film-maker, he had the original play under his arm. 'I thought we might use this as a guide,' he said. 'Fine,'

Views of Berlin: *A Foreign Affair* and *One, Two, Three*

Preminger's Kommandant

said Wilder, dropping it to the floor, 'we'll use it as a doorstop.'

'Billy enjoys life more than anybody I know,' says Walter Reisch. 'Of course, he's cruelly rude. He has very little leniency. But that's not from success. His wife once said, "Long before Billy Wilder was Billy Wilder, he behaved as though he were Billy Wilder." '

While discussing the inevitable doomsday, 'when TV or fallout, whichever turns out more lethal,' has brought man back to the cave, Wilder was asked how man would eat . . . what he would do for a living. 'We will be living by selling each other Utrillos and pre-Columbian dogs.' It was Wilder who coined the sentence, 'Let me get out of these wet clothes and into a dry martini,' although the ad-lib is always attributed to Robert Benchley. If his brain is full of razor-blades, it is also a top-sync transmission because Wilder can switch metaphors in mid-air and has a passion for avoiding the obvious.

Nobody escapes Wilder's acerbity. Audrey, a former singer with the Tommy Dorsey Band, whom Reisch describes as 'brilliant, beautiful and as hard as he is,' is fifteen years younger than he, and on their first wedding anniversary got up in the morning and found him reading *The Hollywood Reporter* at breakfast. He did not look up as she came dewy-eyed into the room. 'Do you know what day this is, dear?'

'June thirtieth,' Wilder said.

'It's our anniversary,' she said, pouting.

'Please,' Billy grimaced, 'not while I'm eating.'

Like many wives, Audrey gives him lists of gifts when he goes places. When he was in Paris for *Irma la Douce* exteriors, she said she wanted some Charvet ties for a friend of hers to give her husband; and, she added, 'ever since I first went to Paris, I've wanted a bidet of my own.' Wilder frowned and said he might have trouble getting a bidet, but he would try. A few days later, a cable came back. CHARVET TIES ON WAY STOP BIDET IMPOSSIBLE OBTAIN STOP SUGGEST HANDSTAND IN SHOWER. When Audrey was his prospective wife, he is supposed to have stretched his love declaration to yet unheard of heights of poetic romanticism by saying: 'I'd worship the ground you walk on if you lived in a better neighbourhood.'

Other Wilder quotes:

On his own films: 'There are some I loathe less than others.'

On critics: 'What they call dirty in our pictures, they call lusty in foreign films.'

On mise en scène: 'Anyone who enters a room not through a door but through a window already is a centre of interest, right?' 'The New Wave, you watch, will discover the slow dissolve in ten years or so.'

On France: 'It is a place where the money falls apart and yet you can't tear the toilet-paper.'

On English and his mastery thereof: 'If you think I have an accent, you should have heard Lubitsch. But he had a wonderful feeling for American idiom and dialogue. As Van Gogh said, you either have an ear or you don't.'

Wilder's English has been the object of scholarly studies and continuous awe. His own explanation is prosaic: 'When I arrived in the U.S., I couldn't speak a word of English. Well, let's say I knew a dozen words the Production Code Office wouldn't tolerate. I learned by not associating myself with the European refugee colony, by going around with new American friends, by listening to the radio. Perhaps it helps you to learn the language if you go into it cold. It pours into you and stays.'

Wilder has never gone 'Hollywood'. He does not call people 'Baby' or 'Pussycat', but is more apt to say Mr Watson or Mr Green in the ironic, formal manner of a college professor. He cares little about personal publicity, except as it will help a film, and has no public relations man and no agent. When I told him that this book was being written, he recommended Richard Lemon's thorough feature on him in the *Saturday Evening Post* and, mellowing only slightly at the end, said he hoped the book wouldn't be too tough on him.

Summing up his own life, he says:

'When I was first trying to get into the movies in Berlin, I lived in a rooming house. Next to my room was the can, and in it was a toilet that was on the blink. The water kept running all night long. I would lie there and listen to it and since I was young and romantic, I would imagine that it was a beautiful waterfall—just to get my mind off the monotony of the thought of it being the can. Now we dissolve to twenty-five years later and I'm finally rich enough to take a cure at Badgastein, the Austrian spa where there is the most beautiful waterfall in the whole world. There I am in bed, listening to the waterfall. And after all I've been through, all the trouble and all the money I've made—all the awards and everything else—there I am in that resort and all I can think of is that goddamned Berlin toilet. That, like the man says, is the story of my life.'

18

Wilder shooting *Irma la Douce*

2: Chronology

'If people loved each other more, they'd shoot each
other less.'
'Are you a religious fanatic or something?'
                                        Love in the Afternoon

'He is a tall, loose-jointed man of forty with a brain full of razor-
blades.' This description of a character in *The Fortune Cookie*
script is also, reportedly, a description by William Holden of Billy
Wilder.

There has never been a shortage of descriptions of Wilder. He
has been called a Rasputin on celluloid, a poor man's Rilke, the
misanthrope who can only see the bad side and must make a sick
joke of it, the mixer of acid and *l'eau de rose*, in short, a man hating
people for fun and profit.

Billy Wilder is about Hollywood's only *auteur*. He is a film-
maker who has written, although always with collaborators, every
film he has made, and since 1959 he has had full control—artistic
and otherwise—over his work. Sometimes dedicated to turning
out handcrafted bawdy comedies, sometimes to digging into the
intransigent humanity of the American human, Wilder has
managed to average an Academy Award every five years. His films
have grossed an estimated $80 million, and he has been fêted with
retrospectives and festivals the world over.

Wilder, who has no personal prints of his films and no leather-
bound editions of his screenplays, is an author because of a point
of view—an exact, adroit and sardonic one, to be sure. In the
stage play *Stalag 17*, the hero was a beaten, spiritless, albeit funny
man who rose to heights only when his patriotism and sense of
honour were outraged. Wilder's *Stalag 17* had a hero who was a

Wilder heroes: Holden's hardboiled heckler in *Stalag 17*
and Lemmon on the way to the top in *The Apartment*

hardboiled heckler amassing a fortune in silk stockings, cigarettes, bottles of wine and clocks by pandering to the lowest taste of his fellow prisoners-of-war. He arranged a horse-race with mice (not in the play); he built a distillery (not in the play); and he built a telescope, not for planning escape but for peeping into the women's barracks (not in the play). The moral of *The Apartment* is that social success is only possible at the cost of the lowest compromises. At the fade-out, Jack Lemmon and Shirley MacLaine will be happy—but jobless.

'Wilder is the most precise, indeed relentless, chronicler of the post-war American, in shade as well as in light, that the motion picture has produced,' said curator Richard Griffith in opening a New York Museum of Modern Art Retrospective on Wilder.

'He has always been the way he is today,' says Reisch. 'He was never sentimental, he was always fearless . . . even when he had nothing. He was sassy and aggressive; he would rather have lost a job than compromised or said yes. And he did lose jobs. He made himself unpopular in the early days—he was overbearing and arrogant and still is today in some ways.'

Samuel Wilder was born in Vienna, 22 June 1906. The sunset years of the Habsburg Empire of his childhood and the feverish and disillusioned post-war Berlin bohemia of his youth have marked him as much as his Jewish origin.

His father, Max Wilder, is a hotel-owner who flits from business to business: owner of a trout-hatchery and a watch-factory, operator of restaurants and exporter of leather handbags. Hoping that Samuel will be a lawyer, he sends his son to the Real Gymnasium and has him enrol at the University of Vienna. The academic career lasts less than a year, however, and Wilder gets a job at *Die Stunde* as a reporter. For one Christmas issue, he interviews Sigmund Freud, Alfred Adler, Richard Strauss and Arthur Schnitzler, all in one morning.

But the magnet of the post-war German-speaking world is Berlin, and like so many young intellectuals of the broken-up Austro-Hungarian Empire, Wilder lusts for the irresistible melting-pot of the 'aware people' of the 1920s. A favourable review of

German night life: *Witness for the Prosecution*

Paul Whiteman's 'symphonic jazz orchestra' Vienna concert allows Wilder to go to Berlin, where he goes to work for Berlin's biggest afternoon tabloid, *B.Z. am Mittag*, for which Erich-Maria Remarque also works. Wilder's next career is something often classified as a ballroom-dancer, but he scorns the euphemism. 'I was a gigolo, dancing for a while at the Eden Hotel. I served as a tea-time partner for lonely ladies.'

On the side, Wilder writes scripts and tries to elbow himself into the cinema. He gets his first break through a happy series of circumstances. The daughter of his landlord is married to a six-foot Prussian nightclub owner, who snores. To console herself, she picks playmates who have more gallantry, if less money, and one night her husband inevitably comes home too early. Billy becomes aware of a man on the ledge outside his window—a man who obviously has no intention of going back into the room to defend his paramour against the husky husband and instead knocks on Wilder's window.

Wilder recognises the man as a well-known producer. Seeing that the man has nothing to do for the moment but listen to the sound of exploding tempers in the next room, Wilder presses one of his scripts on him. The man sighs, and according to some versions of this edifying story, signs a contract on the spot. Other variants have it that Wilder lets the producer into his room before thrusting the script on him. The story ends with the cuckolder leaving by Wilder's door to the accompaniment of the neighbour's snoring.

During the next four years, Wilder writes about twenty pictures, the first being the minor classic *Menschen am Sonntag* (*People on Sunday*), a late silent film which grouped the talents of Robert Siodmak, Eugen Schüfftan, Edgar Ulmer, Fred Zinnemann, Moritz Seeler and Wilder. Conceived, if not actually written, at the Romanisches Café, Berlin's celebrated artists' hangout in the 1920s, the film was shot on Sundays for 5,000 inflation Reichsmarks and was a convincing portrait of Berlin's 'little people', a salesgirl, a travelling salesman, a movie extra and a chauffeur, 'spending their Sundays at a lake, bathing, cooking, lying about on the beach, making futile contact with each other and people like them,' as Siegfried Kracauer describes it.*

Wilder is having dinner at the Kempinski Hotel when the Reichstag burns, and when Hitler comes to power in February 1933, Wilder, together with Reisch, lights out for Paris. 'It seemed the wise thing for a Jew to do,' is his laconic comment years later.

Paris is less hospitable than Berlin. Wilder scrounges, living off the German-Jewish expatriates who have money to lend, enduring the days in a sour little hotel in what he later termed 'dignified starvation'. He continues to peddle scripts and gets to co-direct, with Alexander Esway, *Mauvaise Graine*, the first of six pictures that Danielle Darrieux makes in 1933.†

Mauvaise Graine is a second assignment as director for Esway, a Hungarian-born former actor who makes a minor career in France directing half a dozen films, including several Fernandel comedies and *Education de Prince* with Louis Jouvet and Elvire Popesco, before his death in 1947. Written by Wilder and H. G. Lustig, a reporter confrère of Wilder's from Berlin, *Mauvaise Graine* is based on a story by Wilder. The picture brings Wilder to

---

* Kracauer, *From Caligari to Hitler*, Dobson, 1947.
† One of the other five is *La Crise est Finie*, directed by Robert Siodmak.

the attention of fellow expatriate Joe May, who likes an original screen treatment of Wilder's, *Pam-Pam*. May takes it with him to Hollywood, where it is bought by Columbia but never produced. Their money transports Wilder to Hollywood, via Mexico, but things are even tougher in Glamourland than in Paris.

Possessing little money, less English and no job, the fearless screenwriter lives for several weeks in an empty ladies' room at Chateau Marmont, an actors' hotel on Sunset Strip, then runs into Peter Lorre and moves in with him for fifty cents a day. Wilder attacks the problem of survival by writing two original scripts in German. Translated, they go unsold. Two years of this advanced state of penury follow, but through this stretch of rejection and failure, Wilder gains an astonishingly good grip of what is henceforth to be his native tongue. He keeps the family back home informed by sending clippings about Thornton Wilder, explaining that publishers insist on his having a classier name.

After these low-calorie years of occasional co-writing jobs, Wilder marries the daughter of a prominent California attorney and gets a writing job at Paramount—a studio which at that time employs so many refugees that the Writers Building is called the Tower of Babel. Wilder makes little initial impression and he is seriously studying the 'Want Ads' when, at the whim of a producer, he is teamed with Charles Brackett, a suave New England Yankee.

Their association is to give American cinema some of its best films of the late 1930s and 1940s. But, for the time being, it is scripts in the tradition of the Viennese operas, fitting the studio's Depression policy of escapist entertainment set in European high-life—stories about millionaires, chambermaids, assassins, drunkards, smart-alec cab-drivers and *nouveaux riches*. Their most famous joint screenplay is *Ninotchka* for Ernst Lubitsch, which has Greta Garbo as a Russian commissar corrupted by Western perfumes and dazzling playboys.

The genre ceases to amuse with the outbreak of the Second World War, and Wilder and Brackett chart its disappearance in

The monkey funeral: Stroheim and Swanson in *Sunset Boulevard*

scripts for two films directed by Mitchell Leisen—*Arise My Love*, set against a collapsing Europe, and *Hold Back the Dawn*, in which a gigolo (Charles Boyer) is discovered trying to get into the United States via Mexico by marrying an American school-teacher.

Wilder's first pictures as a director are *The Major and the Minor* and *Five Graves to Cairo*, both written with Brackett. Wilder's passion for touching raw nerves and spilling illusion and cynicism grows as the box-office successes make the Wilder-Brackett duo untouchable. *Double Indemnity* is termed 'a blueprint for perfect murder' by the Hays Office, a seedy drama set in a shabby Los Angeles bungalow and a hideous insurance office. The vision of New York in *The Lost Weekend* remains among the most unsparing ever recorded on film, a nightmare of litter-strewn streets, a cluttered apartment looking out to a desolate stone wilderness, the elevated train clanging across Third Avenue in the dirty light of a summer morning. But even this harsh look at alcoholism is a success, and Wilder and Brackett can do no wrong.

The Emperor Waltz, a twist of old Viennese corn written for Bing Crosby, is their first flop and they hurry into a sharp piece of merchandise—*A Foreign Affair*—in which Wilder finds loads of laughs in an unlikely place, at least for 1947, the ruins of Berlin. They follow up with their masterpiece, *Sunset Boulevard*. In this tale of old Hollywood with cockroaches in the interstices, and the new Glamourland, stupefyingly vulgar and brash, Wilder burns images into celluloid that stick in the mind's eye years after. 'Curiously,' noted Bosley Crowther at the time, 'even this sharp and corrosive film has a great popular appeal.'

But Wilder and Brackett split up after *Sunset Boulevard*, and *Ace in the Hole*, Wilder's first solo, is his starkest. The film purports to attack sensationalism—the brutal way in which Press and carnival promoters exploit the sudden burial of a man in a New Mexico cave. A reporter (Kirk Douglas) who has fallen from 'the big time' sees the chance for a return to the top in this buried alive story. He plays it out, keeping the excitement whipped up for a week, and deliberately delays the rescue on the sound theory that the golden goose is not yet ready to be killed. The film has no cliff-hanging happy ending. The buried man dies and his widow turns on the reporter and stabs him to death. Another director might have made the audience feel the agony of the man in the cave and his increasing sense of hopelessness; but Wilder concentrates on the crowd above, a collective monster erecting a carnival over the tomb—a Ferris wheel, hot-dog stands, TV cameras, a Press tent, and a new popular hit, 'We're Coming, Leo', in honour of the man in the hole.

The film very nearly entombs Wilder himself. Resistance to the picture is so great that Paramount has to change the title to *The Big Carnival* and send persuasive publicity agents round city desks to explain that Wilder meant no sweeping insult to the gentlemen of the Press. Nothing helps. It isn't the Press that doesn't like the image of itself, but the public.

The film is a box-office disaster, but Wilder goes right on turning the Broadway hit, *Stalag 17*, into a raucous prisoner-of-war camp comedy that is banned in Germany for six years and in

Ace in the Hole: The Big Carnival →

Trauner's Old Bailey: *Witness for the Prosecution*

Spain for eleven years. With *Sabrina*, Wilder changes gears, and presenting the screen's most incongruous duo—Audrey Hepburn and Humphrey Bogart—manages to show that love and money mix readily. And with his screen version of George Axelrod's marital comedy, *The Seven Year Itch*, he goes on to prove that nothing really adulterous has to happen in a Wilder film. The shooting of both films involves monumental personality conflicts, with Wilder ready to kill Bogart at one point and Marilyn Monroe throwing her major tantrums.

Wilder himself calls the $6 million flop *The Spirit of St. Louis* 'a bad decision', and goes overseas to shoot *Love in the Afternoon*, an expensive Lubitsch imitation which goes over budget because it is shot in expensive exteriors in suburban Paris. And for *Witness for the Prosecution*, he stays at home and has Alexander Trauner build a $75,000 replica of the Old Bailey on Goldwyn Studios' Stage 4. *Some Like It Hot*, made with new Marilyn Monroe flare-ups and a script not finished until four days before shooting ended, is a smash hit, grossing $14 million in America. *The Apartment* is Wilder's most successful 'dirty fairy-tale'—as his new writer, I. A. L. Diamond, calls it. Diamond has worked on the *Love in the Afternoon* screenplay, but not on *Witness for the Prosecution*; but from *Some Like It Hot* to *The Fortune Cookie* this tall and always worried-looking former engineering student is Wilder's writing partner until *The Private Life of Sherlock Holmes*. Wilder and Diamond write the first drafts of this long-planned film, but for the final screenplay, the director turns to his old friend Harry Kurnitz, the stooping, watery-eyed writer of such pictures as *The Man Between* (Carol Reed), and, together with William Faulkner, *Land of the Pharaohs*, besides *Witness for the Prosecution*. A man of legendary wit, Kurnitz died before the Sherlock Holmes film went into production.

Comedy means tempo, Wilder feels, and *One, Two, Three* turns out to be staccato delivery of Cold War punch-lines and a plot in which virtue is punished and corruption and stupidity rewarded. Prostitution is the oldest profession, and writing about it the second oldest. Although the theme has begun to lose something of its morning freshness, Wilder wrings his next two films out of it.

Irma la Douce grosses $18 million in the United States and Canada alone, and *Kiss Me, Stupid* becomes his first taste of failure in seven years. Originally written with Elizabeth Taylor and Charles Laughton in mind, *Irma* is a musicless rendition of the French musical, starring the *Apartment* couple, Shirley MacLaine and Jack Lemmon. *Kiss Me, Stupid*, actually started with Peter Sellers as the jealous songsmith, is set in rural America. Whereas European critics use it as an opportunity to ridicule American manners and mores ('In a world all too obsessively infected with the cult of ghastly good taste, thank heavens for Mr Billy Wilder,' writes the London *Times*), American public and critics are of the opinion that after walking the shaky tightrope between sophistication and salaciousness, Wilder has finally crashed. This story of a seedy songwriter (Ray Walston takes over when Sellers has a near-fatal heart-attack), to whom fate and a detour sign bring Dino (Dean Martin), hit too close to home with

Wilder and bad taste: (*left*) *The Fortune Cookie* and *Some Like It Hot*; (*right*) *Kiss Me, Stupid, The Fortune Cookie* and *One, Two, Three* →

cuckoldry used—in the great American tradition—for the further-ance of free enterprise.

Wilder is unprepared for the onslaught, led by the Catholic Church ('It's hardly more dirty than Joe Levine's blue period, *The Carpetbaggers*,' he says), and needing a box-office hit, he makes another morality play. *The Fortune Cookie* is about 'the familiar, slice-of-life American-style pastime . . . swindling the insurance company,' announces United Artists, and although the film manages several blows at the legal profession, love and mother-hood, it has a virtuous ending.

In 1968, Wilder is planning to make his first film in England—a Wilder version of the Sherlock Holmes adventures. The project dates back to 1957, when Wilder acquired the rights to characters and stories from the Arthur Conan Doyle estate, and initially planned a Broadway musical. The project was plagued by casting problems, however, and Wilder also had difficulty in finding his screen Sherlock and Dr Watson. During pre-production, Peter O'Toole and Peter Sellers are the most frequently mentioned names for the film, which will have little to do with the literary work. 'It will be the friendship between Holmes and Watson when they're young; Iz [Diamond] and I have invented a plot that isn't Doyle's. We only keep the characters and the Baker Street ambiance of turn-of-the-century London.' He set the shooting start of *The Private Life of Sherlock Holmes* for January 1969, with Robert Stephens as the Baker Street sleuth after having seen the actor in the rushes of *The Prime of Miss Jean Brodie*, and with Richard Attenborough named for the role of Dr Watson.

Wilder has a few undone projects. In 1957, he planned an adaptation of Louis Verneuil's comedy *My Sister and I* with Audrey Hepburn in the lead, but the shooting of Fred Zinne-mann's *The Nun's Story* ran over schedule and prior commitments prevented the realisation of this project. Two earlier films that never got made were *Oedipus Rex*, which was to have followed *Ace in the Hole*, and *Pal Joey*, actually made by George Sidney in 1957.

3: Writing

'Shut up and deal.'
　　　　last line in *The Apartment*

'Eighty per cent of a picture is writing,' says Wilder, 'the other twenty per cent is the execution, such as having the camera on the right spot and being able to afford to have good actors in all parts.' Once Wilder quipped that he became a director because he got tired of people 'fouling up my screen stories.' He has also said that the stronger the basic story, the better the jokes play against it. 'I think the funniest picture the Marx Brothers ever made was *A Night at the Opera*, because opera is such a deadly serious background.'

Wilder always writes in collaboration on the theory that two brains work better than one. His collaborators have been called $50,000 secretaries, but Wilder says it all occurs together, 'like playing a piano piece four-handed. After a screenplay is done, it cannot be said that this was his idea, this was mine.'

Wilder's most famous co-author is Charles Brackett, whom he met in 1936 and with whom he made history for Paramount stockholders for the next fourteen years. I. A. L. Diamond has been Wilder's better half since *Some Like It Hot*, but there have also been one-shot collaborators like George Axelrod or Harry Kurnitz, or 'troikas' like Wilder, Samuel Taylor and Ernest Lehman on *Sabrina*, or Wilder, Lesser Samuels and Walter Newman on *Ace in the Hole*.

The Wilder and Brackett typewriters were called Hollywood's foremost hit factories, but Wilder actually hates putting anything

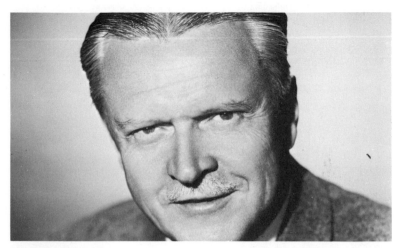

Charles Brackett

on paper. He has an awe for the written work, its finality, and if he could have his way nothing would be put down on paper. Cane or riding-crop in hand, Wilder paces while he thinks and his collaborator sits. Brackett once complained that working with him was like watching a tennis match—it gave him a stiff neck. 'It's such an ordeal to write,' sighs Wilder, 'and such a pleasure to direct.'

In 1931, when George Abbott asks Brackett if he would like to write a picture for Claudette Colbert, the patrician New Englander is a well-established fiction writer for the *Saturday Evening Post*, a novelist and a former *New Yorker* drama critic. Born in 1892 in Saratoga Springs, New York, the son of an eminent lawyer, Brackett studies law at Harvard before drifting into literature during the First World War. The Claudette Colbert picture, *Secrets of a Secretary*, is written in Cuba by Abbott and Brackett in the best tradition of mundane opulence, and Brackett settles down in Hollywood in 1934. After collaborating on ten screenplays, his first solo is the screen adaptation of the Broadway play *Enter Madame*. Directed by Elliott Nugent, the film stars Elissa Landi as the diva and a callow Cary Grant as her leading man.

'Meeting cute': *Bluebeard's Eighth Wife*

Before landing the Paramount job, Wilder has also collaborated on several films. Together with Howard Young, he has written the screen adaptation of the Jerome Kern–Oscar Hammerstein operetta, *Music in the Air*, Joe May's first assignment as director for 20th Century-Fox, starring Gloria Swanson. Together with Franz Schulz, he has turned out the story for the Binnie Barnes starrer, *One Exciting Adventure*, directed by Ernst L. Frank, and co-scripted *Lottery Lover*, directed by fellow Viennese William Thiele. All three films are flops, and with H. S. Kraft, a leading 'jokesmith', Wilder has written the original story for *Champagne Waltz*, directed by A. Edward Sutherland.

Brackett and Wilder are teamed for Lubitsch's *Bluebeard's Eighth Wife*, an adaptation of the French farce by Alfred Savoir. The screenplay is only so-so, but it contains a scene which George Axelrod cites in his play *Will Success Spoil Rock Hunter?*, filmed by Frank Tashlin, as a classic example of hero and heroine 'meeting cute'. Gary Cooper, an American millionaire given to marrying and afflicted by strange economies, is buying pyjamas in a French department store. He tries to buy only the top of the pyjamas when a young Frenchwoman, overhearing his bargaining, offers to buy the lower part of the garment for her father. This 'meeting cute' scene is the first Brackettandwilder Legend. A variation of the legend has it that Wilder came up with the 'meeting cute' idea all by himself, and that producer Arthur Hornblow jun. was intrigued by this offhand inspiration. Aware that Wilder's enthusiastic English revealed significant gaps in grammar and syntax, Hornblow happily remembered that the Writers Building also harboured Brackett, whose polished, elegant prose might have adorned the *New Yorker* but who—like Wilder—was achieving little at the studio. Hornblow decided to combine these dejected talents.

After *Bluebeard's Eighth Wife*, Brackett and Wilder adapt Clifford Goldsmith's high-school play *What a Life*, directed by Ted Reed, and follow with *Midnight*. This screenplay reportedly amuses John Barrymore so much that he asks to read the whole script, not just his lines, when Mitchell Leisen starts to direct it. Next, they go back to work for Lubitsch and, with Reisch as a third team-mate, write *Ninotchka*.

'You didn't see Lubitsch's name on the screen credits as a writer, but he did a lot. We brought the ideas and he added his 'touch'. For example, Brackett, Reisch and I were working for weeks wondering how to show Greta Garbo, the Communist Ninotchka commissar, seduced by capitalism. We had invented many things, and then one day Lubitsch said, "We're going to do it with a hat." So, when you see how in the beginning of the film, arriving together with three commissars, she stops and looks at a rather extravagant hat in a shop window and says, "How can a civilisation survive when women start wearing hats like that! The end of capitalism is near!"—and later in the film, throws the three Russian fellow officials out of her hotel room, closes the door, opens her closet, pulls out the hat from the window, puts it on and sits down at the mirror—that is the Lubitsch touch . . . very simple.'

The outbreak of the Second World War finds Brackett and Wilder scripting *Arise My Love*, a story about an American flier with the Spanish Loyalists, and they follow up with *Hold Back the Dawn*, directed, like *Arise My Love*, by Mitchell Leisen.

The pair are successful, and Hornblow has such faith in them that he occasionally starts a picture with an unfinished script, relying on the twosome to come up with an effective ending. A second Brackettandwilder Legend shows how powerful they are after only five films.

As first written, *Hold Back the Dawn* had Charles Boyer talking to a cockroach. To point up the loneliness of a refugee waiting in a shoddy Mexican border hotel for his chance to get into the United States, Boyer was to say to the cockroach crawling up the wall: 'No, you can't get up there; you haven't got a passport,' and strike the insect from the wall. One day Wilder ran into Boyer, unshaven and in shoddy clothes. 'You must be doing the cockroach scene,' grinned Wilder.

'We have cut the cockroach scene,' replied Boyer loftily. 'People don't talk to cockroaches.' Which was no way to talk to Wilder. He returned to Brackett in icy fury and they decided that for the rest of the script, Boyer wouldn't talk to anyone. After that, all the best scenes went to Olivia de Havilland, and Boyer had little more to do than fill a spot in the background.

After *Hold Back the Dawn*, Brackett and Wilder write *Ball of Fire* for Samuel Goldwyn and Howard Hawks, a comedy thickly inspired by Shaw's *Pygmalion*, which Messrs Goldwyn and Hawks remake—shot for shot—in 1948, calling it *A Song is Born*.

Wilder wants to direct the Brackett-Wilder efforts, and Paramount isn't opposed to the idea. Hornblow gives him his chance with *The Major and the Minor*, an adaptation of Edward Childs Carpenter's escapist comedy that has a disillusioned career woman (Ginger Rogers) dress up in little girl's clothes in order to beat her way back to Iowa from New York on a half-fare ticket. After the war film *Five Graves to Cairo*, follows what they call 'The Year of Infidelities'. While Brackett produces *The Uninvited*, Wilder writes *Double Indemnity* with Raymond Chandler and directs it.

'Billy got so despondent at being without me,' quipped Brackett, 'and so we did *The Lost Weekend*.'

One reason the Wilder-Brackett team was so successful was that they took enough time to think out all the angles and implications of a scene. 'In those days nobody was breathing down their necks and putting pages of script into production as soon as they are written,' is the way an unsigned career story on the pair in *Liberty* magazine sizes them up.* 'After Wilder has acted out every scene in their future production and everything is clear in the last detail, Brackett curls up on the couch and starts to write the script on yellow paper in longhand that can be deciphered only by Miss Hernandez, their secretary. They start out with one hour's work a day and gradually work up to twenty-three hours. This goes on until the screenplay is finished, which takes from four to six months. Every scene, every bit of dialogue, every camera angle is decided in the room. Frequently wild shouts come out of the room and Miss Hernandez closes the window so the neighbours won't listen. Wilder is pacing the floor while Brackett sits in a sofa chair, displaying the lethargy of a graduate of a Yoga school.'

The same style has been carried over to later collaborations, even the mock sensual relationships. During the shooting of *The Fortune Cookie*, Wilder was reminded that this was the seventh time Diamond had been his partner. 'It seems like only the first,' answered Wilder. 'It is a glorious, virginal experience still.'

Why did Wilder and Brackett break up?

The pair became living legends in the mid 1940s. They were known for their ability to work anywhere—in the barber's chair, at parties—and they were known for their no-nonsense attitude towards the industrialists in charge of Hollywood. Where other writers acted like serfs, they stood up for their rights, and eventually were regarded as a pair who could do no wrong. In 1950, at the peak of their partnership, they broke up. 'The Happiest Couple in Hollywood,' as fellow writer Lincoln Barnett called them, got a divorce. Neither has ever said exactly why, and the most likely explanation is simply that Wilder had grown beyond

---

* *Liberty* Magazine, 4 May 1946.

I. A. L. Diamond

the confines of a divided fame. Oddly enough, *Sunset Boulevard* was written after they had decided to terminate their collaboration.

Since their separation, Wilder has, of course, done much better than Brackett, but at first it didn't look that way. While Wilder hit the dust with *Ace in the Hole*, Brackett produced *The Mating Season*, written by him in collaboration with Walter Reisch and Richard Breen, and directed by Leisen. It was an amusing comedy of marital problems and in-law interference, particularly notable for Thelma Ritter's performance in a Marie Dressler-style role. Moving over to 20th Century-Fox as a producer, Brackett wrote— together with Reisch and Breen—20th Century-Fox's last small-screen,* black and white movie, *Titanic*, directed by Jean Negulesco. Few of the following Brackett productions made any box-office marks except *The King and I*, written solo by Ernest Lehman and directed by Walter Lang. Brackett's last films are *Journey to the Centre of the Earth*, and the remake of *State Fair*, directed by José Ferrer in 1962.

Wilder-Diamond screenplays are models of economy. Not an

* 20th Century-Fox began exploiting its CinemaScope patent in 1953.

Wilder and Marilyn

extra 'if', 'and' or 'but' spoil them, and actors rarely want to change a line.

'Both of us sit in the same office, week after week, month after month, five days a week, from nine to six,' says Diamond. 'Then we start working Saturday and Sunday mornings, too. Everything is worked out line by line. In the course of a script, there will be one joke he wants to get in and I'm dead set against it, and vice versa. On plot, we've had knockdown, drag-out fights. It's more or less pre-directed—he knows in the office where he's going to put the camera. We've never started shooting with a complete script. We usually have a third of it to write. We spend three months shooting, three months post-production—editing and scoring—then a short vacation, and we start again.'

Wilder has his own words for not finishing a script before shooting. 'The third act is never finally formulated when we begin shooting,' he grins. 'Our joke is that if you give the bosses the third act in advance, they can fire you any time.'

A final Wilder script makes brilliant reading, and two of the Wilder-Diamond efforts, *Irma la Douce* and *Some Like It Hot*, were published in book form, although Wilder claims he is dead against the practice. 'If you're writing for a director, you give a lot of detail and hope he'll know what you mean. But in our little kitchen, we do both the cooking and the eating. It's from the manufacturer to the consumer.'

'What's difficult is not to find ideas—to make them out of hot air. You get millions of ideas that often have nothing to do with what you want to do. The first big job is to put in the waste-paper basket all the useless ideas,' says Wilder.

Wilder is a stickler for authenticity. The names of many of his characters have been lifted from real life, usually from a famous and inappropriate person. Shirley MacLaine in *The Apartment* got her name, Miss Kubelik, from a violinist; and Marilyn Monroe in *Some Like It Hot* was named Kowalczyk after a Michigan State University football-team half-back. In pursuit of the appearance of reality, Wilder has had many battles with production departments. 'They always try to give you "Lucky Chester" or "Camel Strikes", and I will not stand for that. Or phony names on newspapers, "The N.Y. Blade". Once you have that, you know, all believability goes out the window.'

Which is why James Cagney works for Coca-Cola and not a fictitious soft-drink company in *One, Two, Three* . . . why Jack Lemmon is a CBS-TV cameraman covering a Cleveland Browns football game in *The Fortune Cookie* and why *Sunset Boulevard* is just that. There may be a connection between the desert town's leering name of Climax in *Kiss Me, Stupid* and the fact that the film is one of Wilder's real resounding flops.

Wilder and Diamond came together after Diamond had worked on dozens of screenplays for various studios during fifteen years in Hollywood, and the two men decided they complemented each other perfectly. Diamond—Wilder calls him 'Iz'—started out to be an engineer. Born in Ugheni, Rumania, he came to the United States in 1929 when his father immigrated. Settling in Brooklyn, he attended Columbia University, where he planned to major in mathematics. During his freshman year, he got the writing bug, and with a would-be composer, did the Columbia Varsity Show.

One, Two, Three

The pair went on to establish a record, unequalled even by such famous Columbia graduates as Richard Rodgers, Oscar Hammerstein and Herman Mankiewicz, by writing the next three annual shows.

Diamond joined M-G-M as a junior writer, and after two years with Paramount, made a breakthrough of sorts with a murder musical called *Murder in the Blue Room*, directed by Leslie Goodwins in 1944. He is still an obscure writer, however, when Wilder hires him to collaborate on *Love in the Afternoon* in 1956.

Iz feels his and Wilder's toughest one is *One, Two, Three*, because the world situation was changing faster than they could rewrite their text. 'A playwright can update his lines while his play is running, and a nightclub comedian can adapt his material to the day's headlines. But once a joke is frozen on film, you're stuck with it, come what may,' Diamond wrote in the *New York Times*.*

'It seems rather remote now, but at the time we started writing the script, people were making jokes about Khrushchev pounding his shoe at the U.N. and Castro plucking chickens in his hotel room. As the political climate changed, however, certain subjects that the public had once laughed at suddenly ceased being funny. The invasion of Cuba, the death of Lumumba, Yuri Gagarin's flight—all these events forced revisions in the screenplay.'

'To make the film as up to the minute as possible, we laid the action of the story between June and August 1961—the exact three months when we would be shooting in Germany. The interiors were filmed in Munich . . . and every morning, before leaving for the studio, we would anxiously tune in to hear the latest development in the Berlin crisis. On the afternoon of Saturday, August 12, we arrived in Berlin for the second of our location trips. Early the following morning, we drove out to the Brandenburg Gate and found thousands of West Berliners milling silently along the border, which had been closed the night before.'

When the Berlin Wall went up, Wilder and Diamond had to rewrite large portions of the ending, and they had to build the

---

* *New York Times*, 17 December 1961: '*One, Two, Three*: Timetable Test'.

East side of the Brandenburg Gate at Bavaria Studios' back-lot in Munich.

During production, the Wilder-Diamond association goes on seven days a week. 'It is a luxury now that we can only shoot five days a week, instead of six—as we used to,' says Wilder. 'This means we have serious meetings on Saturdays and Sundays to reconsider what we've done, and rewrite.'

'Giving the average reader a script is like giving him blueprints and asking him to imagine the finished building. You can be as witty as you like in a script, but if it doesn't show on the screen, it doesn't mean a damned thing.'

4: Mise en Scène

'All right, Mr de Mille, I'm ready for my close-up.'
Sunset Boulevard

For a man whose career began by hauling a cuckolder in by the seat of his trousers and blackmailing him ever so gently, Wilder has gone far, and may go further still. Many critics began to write him off after *Ace in the Hole*, as if destructive criticism of people and statements against life were the only way ahead for this most persistently critical film-maker of the English-language cinema. Does turning to comedy necessarily mean selling out?

Wilder's films cost a lot of money, and traditionally satire has been a risky proposition for major distributors. Yet he is about the only big-time American film-maker trying to examine human foibles through wit and corrosive comment.

'They object not to the vulgarity in my art, but the lack of art in my vulgarity,' he says. 'I have been pursued for years by that nasty word—vulgarity. They sit there in the moviehouse and laugh their heads off and then they go out and say "Cheap! Vulgar!" Then they go and see *Pillow Talk* and pronounce it urbane humour. Maybe my work is a little robust but one has to work with what one has. I would be a disaster if I used the sugar-tongs and tried to regiment myself into something unnatural for me.'

'I'm not really a message man. Pictures like *Love in the After-noon* and *Sabrina* are not in any way a comment on the world. Maybe *The Apartment* had a few things to say about society, but it wasn't meant to be a deep-searching exploration of how we are.

On certain levels, once in a while, maybe we smuggle in a little contraband message, but we try never to jump in their faces with our naked pretensions showing because they'll recoil. In certain pictures I do hope they will leave the cinema a little enriched, but I never make them pay a buck and a half and then ram a lecture down their throats.'

If Wilder is banking on chancy ventures, he brings them across with virtuoso delivery. He never tries to woo his audience's consent to his one-joke vision of man; he simply overpowers its resistance with an endless salvo of one-line gags and a prodigal introduction of distorted comic characters, as if he were some latter-day Ben Jonson.

The going is hard in most of Wilder's sweet-sour cocktails, and the comedy is directed that way—hard, clear and ruthless. One of Wilder's idiosyncrasies is to start shooting without finishing the script. The screenplay of *Some Like It Hot* was not completed until four days before the shooting was finished, and the last scene of *The Apartment* was filmed fifteen minutes after the mimeographed pages arrived on the set, with Jack Lemmon and Shirley MacLaine learning their lines from wet Xerox copies.

'It may sound like we don't know what we're doing, but it's not so,' Wilder once explained laboriously. 'We always know where we are going. It's just that we aren't sure how we'll get there . . . until it's time to go.'

Wilder's cardinal rule, the only one he observes 'hard and fast', is never to underestimate the intelligence of the audiences. The second rule is never to bore them.

'To me, a director who uses phenomenal neck-craning set-ups, beautiful pictures everywhere, isn't worth a damn,' Wilder told Richard Gehman.* 'He isn't doing what he should be doing: telling the story.' To Jean Domarchi and Jean Douchet,† he explained that he rarely has any trouble on the set because the film is well prepared. 'When a director hasn't prepared his film well enough, he sometimes has to delete dialogue or sometimes add

---

* In 'Charming Billy', *Playboy*, December 1960.
† *Cahiers du Cinéma* 134, August 1962.

Rehearsal and action: *Irma la Douce*

Wilder and Lemmon: *Irma la Douce*

lines. What he takes away was very important and what he adds is stupid. You have to be prepared.'

Wilder believes that last-minute work on the script affords him a flexibility that helps the actors develop truer interpretations of their parts, and once on the set, he spends more time with his human material than technical details.

'I don't come from the theatre; I haven't studied Max Reinhardt or Lee Strasberg of the Actors' Club [*sic*]. I think I have a pretty good idea of what an actor is, a good ear for dialogue, and I watch out and try not to bore the audience. I'm just a story-teller.'

Wilder's relationship with his actors, on the set and off, is plain and functional, and most of them come back to him should he ever want them a second time round.

'What it all comes down to is selection and taste in the script,' says Jack Lemmon. 'That's the great thing about Billy—he doesn't impose himself before he sees what the actor will bring. And he

Jack Lemmon in *The Apartment*

has an eye and ear like a hawk. Do you remember the scene in *The Apartment* where I come in and just start cleaning up the place, like I'd done it every night for years before? The average director would be afraid to play it like Billy did. They'd say, "Let's get on to more action." But Billy let the scene run two or three minutes. And he invented ideas as he went along. Like when I was cooking, having me straining the spaghetti through a tennis racket. Then he told me that it was just the right touch.'

'Look, suppose someone told you the story-line of *Some Like It Hot*: "Two guys are trying to get away from gangsters and they put on women's clothes, see"—you'd say, "Ah, come on now!" Same with *The Apartment*: "This guy loans out his apartment to his bosses to get ahead in the firm." Sounds corny! But the way Billy handled it! He *sees* the scripts. A script is to be played, not to be read. In his scripts, I can't remember a single word that would have made me feel uncomfortable. With a good script, you get impressed with what they *didn't* write.'

Arlene Francis had a long career behind her as a prime example of American TV womanhood when Wilder cast her as Cagney's wife in *One, Two, Three*, but she felt like a neophyte when she arrived in Berlin. 'The role had nothing to do with my TV personality,' she says. 'Wilder wanted to eradicate that identification completely; he wouldn't even let me wear my diamond heart —which is sort of a trademark. My character was warm and sensible—a woman who had a good marriage—a sort of modern Myrna Loy. Billy sensed I felt like a newcomer. When I arrived, he said, "Now that you're here, we can start." '

Wilder had monumental fights with Marilyn Monroe, and Humphrey Bogart thought William Holden, Audrey Hepburn and Wilder were in cahoots against him during the shooting of *Sabrina*. Fred MacMurray didn't want to play a murderer and resisted Wilder's wooing for several months.

'Shooting *Double Indemnity* was almost effortless after we all got warmed up,' MacMurray recalls. 'Barbara Stanwyck and Edward G. Robinson were fine fellow actors. Wilder gave us what struck me as perfect direction. Once, when I tried to shorten a

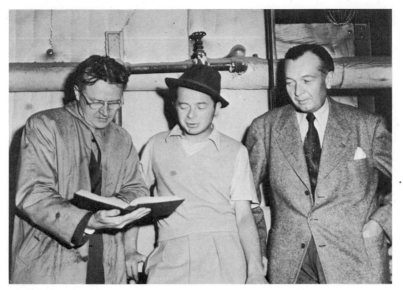

Charles Brackett, Wilder and Doane Harrison

suspense scene, he waved my objections aside. "Stretch it out!" he shouted. I stretched it out, against my better judgement, and it won more favourable comment than any other scene in the picture —which may help to explain why Wilder is a director and I'm just an actor.'

'Billy Wilder is something else again,' says Tony Curtis.

Wilder will tailor scripts to specific actors. When he and Ernest Lehman wrote *Sabrina*, they conceived one part for Cary Grant who, after agreeing to play it, changed his mind. When Bogart took over, Lehman and Wilder began rewriting in a frenzy, staying up most of each night to get a few pages together for the next day. Midway through the shooting, Wilder went to Doane Harrison, his cutter, and asked him to get the electricians to invent some complicated lighting effects for the next scene—something that would take time. When the puzzled Harrison asked why, Wilder said he hadn't written the dialogue yet.

'A movie is a star vehicle,' says Wilder. 'What good is it to have a magnificent concept for which you must have Laurence Olivier and Audrey Hepburn if they're not available?'

The filming of a Wilder movie is relaxed but efficient, and many of his crew members are veterans of other Wilder pictures. Editor Harrison has worked for Wilder for more than twenty-five years, and unlike most cutters, he is always there during shooting to advise and reduce the excess footage. Alexander Trauner has built the sets for nearly every Wilder *opus* since *Love in the Afternoon*; Andre Previn wrote the music for four Wilder movies, Miklos Rozsa for three; Charles Lang jun. was the cinematographer on four Wilder films, and John Seitz on four.

A ruthless innovator of content, Wilder is a classicist of form, defiant and proud of craftsmanship.

'A language had been evolved between the audience and the director,' he says, 'and it is now being replaced by some kind of Esperanto. Dissolves and fades are forgotten; fancy-shmancy shooting is taking over the young directors. There is a madness about camera angles. Helicopter shots, I don't mind—but not in the living-room, please. There is a disregard for neatness in directing. It is dismissed as Hollywood slickness. The Hollywood product is constantly demeaned and insulted, mostly by those who don't see the totality of the Japanese, French or Italian product.'

'I would like to give the impression that the best directing is the one you don't see. The audience must forget that they are in front of a screen—they must be sucked into the screen to the point when they forget that the image is only two-dimensional.'

Wilder uses close-ups sparingly. 'I think a close-up is such a valuable thing—like a trump in bridge.' He likes set-ups with surprises and has been able to afford to have Trauner build sets allowing 360-degree filming. The Rue Casanova set in *Irma la Douce* was the first such set, permitting shooting in any direction, and the Main Street in Climax, Nevada, in *Kiss Me, Stupid* was also an all-round set.

Wilder had resisted colour as long as possible and even dared to make *The Fortune Cookie* in 'a comfortable' black and white. 'I

The Rue Casanova from *Irma la Douce*

Wilder and Gary Cooper: *Love in the Afternoon*

hate colour; even words sound phony when the picture is in colour,' he said once, 'everybody looks blue or red—it's like shooting a jukebox, multicoloured sherbets; it's nauseating.'

He has an even greater aversion for television than for colour, calling it a twenty-one-inch prison. 'I'm delighted with that medium because it used to be that we in films were the lowest form of art. Now we have something to look down on.' Of his own films running on TV, complete with commercials, he has said that if the television networks would have the courtesy to call him up, he might help them cut his films for TV broadcasting. 'How would an author feel if eighty pages were cut out of his novel and every twelve pages there was an underarm deodorant inserted in the text?'

'Pay television is the inevitable answer. When you pay nothing, you get nothing. When you drop some silver in a slot, you are no longer a bored, indifferent audience. You want to see your money's worth or know the reason why.'

Film, feels Wilder, is audience participation and dollars and cents. 'I think the whole idea is to suck the audience in and make them do the work for you . . . make them participate. You have to catch them and they have to be playing with you. It is calculated to look natural. I admire elegant camerawork, but not fancy stuff. Second, it's a matter of dollars and cents. It doesn't have only to do with Hollywood—it has to do with a man's approach to the problem of making those dollars and cents. Look at Fellini. He cleaned up with *La Dolce Vita*. When I saw it, I couldn't decide if it was the greatest or the dreariest picture I'd ever seen, and finally I decided it was both. A remarkable film, excellent because he had stuck to his own principles.'

Wilder, the cynic. Wilder has always been berated for failures of taste and morality. His heroes are seen as sinful weaklings and his stories as below-the-belt satires hooked up with happy endings.

Most writers use Wilder's unorthodoxy to write crisp copy about him ('Wilder is the kind of guy who calls a spade a four-letter word')* and few have bothered to attempt any explanation. The few who have tried have traced his vision of the world back to the childhood and adolescence lived during the last decadent years of the Habsburg Empire. This origin makes him the (youngest) blood-brother of Josef von Sternberg, Fritz Lang, Otto Preminger, Edgar Ulmer, Erich von Stroheim and Max Ophuls, film-makers who seem to see better than others the cracks in the social crust— 'les lézardes des civilisations', as Jean Douchet says†—men who have filled their screens with corrosive and often screechy and mordant mixtures of rose petals floating in acid. The 'Vienna School', nearly all Jewish and bourgeois in origin, puts itself on the screen with Ophuls's *La Ronde*, written by the Arthur Schnitzler interviewed by young Samuel Wilder that morning together with Freud, Adler and Richard Strauss.

'They have in common this pessimistic vision of the world,' says Douchet. 'One can perhaps explain it, at least superficially,

---

* In 'Billy Wilder, Hating People for Fun and Profit' by Jim Murray, *Los Angeles Magazine*, October 1963.
† *Cahiers du Cinéma* 113, November 1960.

by the fact that their childhood was spent in a society in full decadence. . . . More lucid than others, they see the cracks in a civilisation in all its splendour; they don't have to forgive weaknesses, nor do they have to excuse them. On the contrary, they denounce them violently. They know that man is evil because the structures of society force him to be so. Man must, therefore, be chastised in order to bring back in him a desire for nobler values.'

But Lubitsch, Wilder's avowed master, was a Berliner, and Wilder spent his formative years in the effervescent capital of the Weimar Republic, the crucible of disenchantment. From the savage art of George Grosz to Bertolt Brecht's scathing plays, the Berlin bohemia of the 1920s reflected only bitterly upon man's essential, constitutional foolishness.

Yet, in retrospect, Wilder feels that the American literary 'lost generation' influenced him more than Grosz, Brecht and other regulars at the Romanisches Café. Wilder knew Brecht, as he knew Thomas Mann, Franz Werfel and Max Brod (Luigi Pirandello also spent a better part of his Berlin years at the Romanisches Café), but read Upton Sinclair and Sinclair Lewis. 'If I was influenced by anybody it was von Stroheim and Lubitsch. However, I don't believe any of that "intellectual stimulus" crap. Take Confucius—he said some pretty stimulating things, but he never got to Paris in his life.'

The romance between Wilder and Hollywood, now in its second quarter-century, is one of the enduring love-affairs of the West, and he is one of the few who go on cherishing the Californian dream-factory. 'I like it here; I feel comfortable; I work with my friends. What more do you want?'

Wilder has even become a little possessive about the movie community, and he takes umbrage at those who disparage or mistreat it. When Darryl Zanuck took over at 20th Century-Fox in 1963 and let go a number of veterans, including one of Wilder's former associates, Wilder told him in a telegram released to the Press that the firings were callous and his studio should be razed. When screenwriter Abby Mann spoke critically of Hollywood at a Moscow Film Festival, Wilder shot wires at *Daily Variety* and *The*

Wilder demonstrates hospital bedmaking: *The Fortune Cookie*

Hollywood Reporter asking who appointed Abby Mann as spokesman for the American Film World in Moscow.

This love for his adopted city has made him dish out some snarling comment on European films and filming, but he has also acknowledged that American film-makers can thank European critics for being known at all.

'As for freedom, all the Mirisch Company asks me is a vague outline of the story and who's going to be in it. The rest is up to me; can you get more freedom than that?' The relationship with the Mirii, as the brothers are colloquially known, has been cordial, and Wilder was once moved to call Harold, Marvin and Walter, plus their elder brother Irving, a stockholder in the company, Papa Max, their father now in his nineties, and a son of Marvin on the legal staff, 'The Magnificent Seven' after one of their better films. In 1968, however, Wilder contemplated making films for others.

5: The Six with Brackett

The Major and the Minor is comedy in the escapist vein of the early war years with a frothy coating of patriotism and 'doing our duty'. 'Like most engaging screen comedies, *The Major and the Minor* is as intent upon incidental nonsense as it is on straight story outline,' wrote the *New York Herald Tribune*. 'Since Miss Rogers takes a tremendous stride toward becoming the most versatile and captivating actress in films and a director with a fresh viewpoint has gone to town, *The Major and the Minor* is an enchanting film farce.'*

With Arthur Hornblow jun. as their producer, Wilder and Brackett had written a sassy screenplay based on Edward Childs Carpenter's play and a *Saturday Evening Post* story by Fannie Kilbourne, and proved again that they could turn anything into gold. The play *Connie Goes Home* had not been successful; the more cleverly titled film was a handsome hit.

The idea of having a disillusioned career woman in New York dress up in little girl's clothes in order to beat her way back to Iowa on a half-fare railway ticket was a good one, and the Wilder-Brackett screenplay proved, in the words of *Daily Variety*, that 'children playing grown-ups isn't half as much fun as a grown-up playing a kid'.†

* *New York Herald Tribune*, 20 September 1942.
† *Daily Variety*, 28 August 1942.

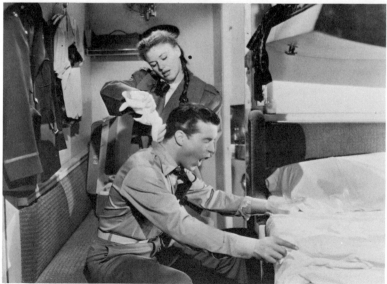

The Major and the Minor: Ginger Rogers and Ray Milland

Playing Susan Applegate without make-up—a fact fan maga-zines duly noted—Ginger Rogers (who had just won an Oscar)[*] and Wilder filled nearly every sequence with captivating capers, beginning with the train conductor becoming suspicious and she seeking refuge in the compartment of Ray Milland, an Army Major stationed at a boys' military school. The Major's solicitous comforting of the supposedly frightened Sue-Sue, as she calls herself when she reverts to the age of twelve, is a hilarious sequence showing that Hornblow was right in giving Wilder a chance to direct. Never suspecting her real age, the Major naturally insists on her sleeping in the lower berth rather than sitting up all night in the day coach. Susan is found there the next morning by the Major's fiancée (twenty years later, Wilder would probably have made her a wife), and has to continue her masquerade at the boys' military school to provide him with a cover story.

Wilder milks all the fun he can out of the college. The pre-cocious cadets prove to be more wolfish than any executive Romeo Susan had ever met in wicked New York, and it is, of course, a real child (Diana Lynn) who sees through the heroine's deception. The film is somewhat careful in tone, but when Ginger Rogers is hiring a stumble-bum to impersonate her father, and playing deadpan with the Major to let him fumble through a lecture on the facts of life, it has a gaiety which is hard to resist. As the worldly-wise cadets, a whole batch of amusing performances are delivered, and the boys' discussion of the Maginot Line tactics was singled out in trade reviews as 'a surefire routine'. Milland plays the role of the muddle-headed Major with a feeling for caricature, and Diana Lynn is excellent as the child seeing through the deception but protecting Susan in order to cross up her predatory elder sister (Rita Johnson), who wants to keep her fiancé from fighting the war. Mrs Lola Rogers makes an appear-ance as the screen mother of her real daughter.

The Major and the Minor, in fact, is everything a freshman director can hope for: good reviews and better box-office returns, allowing him to forge ahead. The film had a home-front martial

---

[*] For her performance in Sam Wood's *Kitty Foyle*.

background with the Major eager to go into active service. What about a real war picture?

The Major and the Minor was the last film on Hornblow's Paramount contract, and when he left for M-G-M, Brackett found himself appointed producer. *Five Graves to Cairo* is the first W & B endeavour over which the pair have absolute control.

Five Graves to Cairo is an espionage thriller taking place in the desert wastes of Libya after the fall of Tobruk in 1942. It was in the can by 2 February 1943—three months *before* Field-Marshal Erwin Rommel lost Tunis and his Afrika Korps was forced to fall back on Sicily. W & B also knew how to be fast.

The idea of making Rommel's still-raging Africa campaign into an exciting potboiler belonged to Lajos Biro, but the idea of having Erich von Stroheim incarnate the Field-Marshal was Wilder's, although biographers of von Stroheim claim he was only a last choice after Paramount had screened a dozen actors.[*] Biro was another native of the Austro-Hungarian Empire, a writer of several Lubitsch comedies, including the Pola Negri starrer, *Forbidden Paradise*, 1942. A friend of Alexander Korda, Biro had written the *Private Life of Henry VIII* script with him, and before he died in 1948 wrote *A Royal Scandal* for Otto Preminger. Biro had written an espionage scenario set in the First World War for Pola Negri, but Wilder and Brackett sat up and listened when he suggested an updating to the current war.

A solitary British tank rolls over the dunes without guidance: all of the crew are dead, with one exception. Franchot Tone plays the sole survivor, who crawls into a town on the Libyan border only to discover that his regiment has left and the Germans have moved in. The town's hostelry is run by its Egyptian owner (Akim Tamiroff) and an Alsatian maid (Anne Baxter), who have remained after other members of the staff fled with the British. When the officer arrives, they decide at first to turn him over to the invaders, but later agree to give him shelter. A crippled manservant has been

[*] Peter Noble: 'Stroheim—His Work and Influence', *Sight and Sound*, Winter 1947–48.

killed in a recent air raid, and it is decided that Tone should assume this man's identity. When Rommel (von Stroheim) sets up his General Staff Headquarters in the hostelry, Tone discovers that the cripple he impersonates was in the pay of the Nazis.

With considerable self-esteem, the Field-Marshal divulges that five years before the war, the Germans had hidden large supplies of petrol, ammunition and water in the sandy wastes, and that the key to these caches is in the five letters spelling out 'Egypt' on the map. It is now Tone's task to get the information that the Germans are not relying upon supply-lines to the British in Cairo, and the plot spins about whether or not the German plan to use the 'five graves to Cairo' will be successful. The Alsatian maid, finally convinced that her brother, killed at Dunkirk, had not been deserted by the British, crosses to the Allied side and sacrifices her life to help the hero.

Surprisingly, for such a dynamic picture, there is a minimum of actual battle scenes in *Five Graves to Cairo*, shot at Salton Sea near Indio, California, a wildlife refuge at the southern end of the Mojave Desert. Three of the principals—Tone, Tamiroff and Fortunio Bonanova, the last playing a harassed Italian attached to the Rommel Staff—made private 16 mm colour movies. After a spectacular battle scene, Wilder shouted 'Good!', then turned to the three amateurs hard at work and politely asked, 'How was it for you, gentlemen? Shall we print it?'

The film was a success, and von Stroheim's incarnation of Rommel was singled out both in reviews and publicity as 'the man you love to hate'. Brackett saw *Five Graves to Cairo* on television in 1959 and called it 'a topnotch melodrama on which hangs a dreadful smell of propaganda.' Also, the British dialogue he and Wilder had devised for Franchot Tone made him squirm. 'I realise how wise Somerset Maugham has always been in refusing to write American dialogue.'

After *Double Indemnity* (see next chapter), Wilder made *The Lost Weekend*, the film which, at the age of thirty-eight, brought him into the top class of directors. 'It was after this picture that

Five Graves to Cairo: Fortunio Bonanova, Franchot Tone, von Stroheim, Peter Van Eyck

Ray Milland, Doris Dowling and bartender Howard da Silva: *The Lost Weekend*

people started noticing me,' he said. 'Oddly,' reminisced Brackett, '*The Lost Weekend* was the easiest script we wrote, thanks to the superb novel.'

Charles R. Jackson's provocative novel about an alcoholic was not pleasant. Neither was the film, shot during the fall of 1944, and Paramount was apprehensive about it. 'The studio was against it right from the start, but the trade reviews were favourable and it eventually turned into one of those oddball successes that you only have once every ten years or so,' says Wilder. Representatives of the whisky interests protested on the grounds that any depiction of a five-day binge would prejudice audiences against their product. At the same time, Prohibition groups protested on the grounds that it would incite drinking. Wilder and Brackett ignored them, as well as other representatives of these same groups. The whisky interests announced that a film like *The Lost Weekend* would be a great boon to producers of the better brands, for Don

Birnam drinks the cheapest stuff he can buy, and the Prohibitionists were happy because the film was a lesson on the evils of drink. Brackett and Wilder never quite made up their minds themselves whether the film made a plea for temperance or not.

Ray Milland's portrayal of Don Birnam, the pitiful, congenital drunk, was the best performance so far in his career, and he had to live with it for years. In a *Life* interview two years after the shooting,* he told of a harrowing hangover—of incidents of barkeepers, sailors and passers-by taunting and ridiculing him, of columnists inventing constant gags like 'Milland has invented a new type of home bar.' There were also pathetic letters from drunks.

Wilder experimented with pace in *The Lost Weekend*—in slowness and not, as in *One, Two, Three* sixteen years later, in staccato delivery. *The Lost Weekend* is slowly paced to enhance the dramatic effect of this weekend of Birnam fighting his craving in some of his calmer moments, then yielding. When he succumbs, nothing stands in his way. He pilfers money left for the housemaid, tries to sell his typewriter, attempts to steal a wallet in a cocktail lounge. Finally, he pawns his girl's coat to buy back a gun. The girl (Jane Wyman) persuades him not to shoot himself, and he hits the sawdust trail. The redemption—not in the book—is not altogether convincing and cuts into the structure of the stern and hard realism, just as Birnam's spilling all the discouragement and shattered dreams of his life to a bartender is too long and out of tune.

The Lost Weekend has exteriors shot in New York, a novelty Wilder fought hard for. In the book, Birnam's desperate journey to hawk his typewriter was along Second Avenue, a mistake Jackson later admitted. Birnam should have walked up Third Avenue, the great pawnshop, and Wilder shot the 'long walk' on Third Avenue with cameras hidden in laundry trucks and empty stores. During the three weeks filming, Milland was recognised only once. The whiff of anti-Semitism in Jackson's book is kept intact, and all the pawnshops are still closed because it is

* *Life,* 11 March 1946.

Third Avenue and cocktail lounge: *The Lost Weekend*

Yom Kippur the day Birnam chooses to carry his portable from one block to another. In the film, he walks fifty blocks before he discovers it is a Jewish holiday.

At the end of the same day, Birnam falls down a flight of stairs, which leads to one of the grimmest of movie scenes: the Bellevue Hospital Alcoholic Ward. When the lights in the ward go out and the screams go up, Wilder treats his audiences to the full force of the horrors of delirium tremens. 'Last week was very heavy,' says the male nurse (Frank Faylen). 'One night we took in twenty. Usually they come in between three in the afternoon and eight in the morning.'

'Wilder's a tough man to follow,' recalls George Seaton, who tried to shoot several sequences of *The Miracle on 34th Street* (titled *The Big Heart* in Britain) at Bellevue. 'The hospital manager practically threw me out because he was still mad at himself for having given Wilder permission to shoot at the hospital. What made him particularly angry was that the picture showed a male nurse brutalising an alcoholic.'

The Lost Weekend was a daring film in 1945. Alcoholism as such had not been treated on the screen before and the film did nothing to sugarcoat the grim tale of a man tortured by drink. It did not preach, just stated a case.

During the shooting, the studio, newspapers and friends of the principals were against it. The *Los Angeles Times* felt Wilder was risking his future,* financial and artistic, and friends of Milland said he was committing professional suicide. But once the film was released, the tune changed. *Life* called it 1945's best movie, and *The Lost Weekend* took four Academy Awards—to the film itself for being the year's best, to Milland for acting, to Wilder for directing, and to Wilder and Brackett for writing the best screenplay.

Wilder, shooting his first colour film, dwarfs later tales of Antonioni painting a few vegetables for his colour début in *The Red Desert* or Visconti having television aerials torn down in a village for *The Leopard*. Exteriors for *The Emperor Waltz* were

---

* *Los Angeles Times*, 3 December 1944.

Joan Fontaine, Bing Crosby with (*below*) Roland Culver and (*right*) puppy offspring: *The Emperor Waltz*

shot in the Canadian Rockies, and here—with the Master commenting himself—is a description of what was done to film two dogs in a two-minute scene. Wilder had a whole side of a mountain painted ('not that we disagreed with nature, but Technicolor is sometimes a little harder to please'). He added new trees to the landscape ('the old ones were in the wrong places'), built an island supported by gigantic gas-filled drums in the middle of Lake Leach, repainted highways ('roads are always either too dark or too light'), imported 4,000 daisies from California and then painted them blue ('white photographs too glaringly')—all for a scene during which two dogs meet, bite and fall in love. Cost—$90,000.

This re-creation in the Jasper National Park with the Rockies doubling for the Alps supported a fey tale about an American palace-to-palace phonograph salesman named Smith, who in 1901 goes to Austria with the idea of selling the new invention to

Emperor Franz Josef (Richard Haydn). Bing Crosby plays the Yank at Schönbrunn who falls in love during working hours.

The plot-line has Smith taking with him an engaging and talented His Master's Voice type of fox-terrier. The latter forms an attachment for a pedigree poodle belonging to a beautiful countess (Joan Fontaine); friendship ripens into love, upsetting the Emperor's plans for a canine *mariage de convenance*. A parallel romance develops between the dog-owners, and the whole charade proves that true love, canine or human, is a democratic institution capable of transcending convention, social position and geographical barriers.

The Emperor Waltz is Wilder and Brackett's first taste of defeat. The lavish production is only moderately and spasmodically amusing, and despite a hard-sell campaign by Paramount, the film fails. It does contain Wilder's first piece of dashing *mise en scène*: an opening ballroom sequence which is a bang-up piece of burlesque of Viennese romance, combining splendour, lightness and smart movie-making. But, as Bosley Crowther summed it up, the picture is 'nothing more than a dash of *The Prisoner of Zenda*, a twist of old Vienna "corn" and plenty of any "roadshow".'*

With *A Foreign Affair*, Wilder finds laughter in an unlikely place—the ruins of Berlin. Shot during the winter of 1947–48, this satirical probe of just how many favours a GI could buy with a candy-bar in the ruins of Europe is a sharp piece of merchandise, sleek and impatient. The U.S. Congress did not like *A Foreign Affair*, and the Defence Department found the film a shade embarrassing since it satirised regulations and officialdom in a smooth and sly manner.

The story, written by Wilder, Brackett and Richard Breen, is about the 'moral malaria' allegedly infecting the 12,000 U.S. troops in Berlin and causing a Congressional Committee to investigate. Congresswoman Jean Arthur, looking suspiciously like Claire Booth Luce complete with braids and briefcase, comes to Berlin and has her spinster soul shocked by the amount of fraternising between GIs and Herrenvolk. Events leading to her

* *New York Times*, 27 June 1948.

Jean Arthur, Marlene Dietrich and (*below*) John Lund: *A Foreign Affair*

discovery that you can't pin an archangel's stripes on a sergeant in charge of morale are among the most hilarious moments. Another savage highlight is a scene in which she learns some embarrassing things about what the occupiers think of the folks back home. She gets her man (John Lund), but there is a big question as to who is the luckiest in the end, when Marlene Dietrich is herded off to de-Nazification jail by a fair-sized army. Arthur and Dietrich play their roles to the hilt, reaching their peak in a scene where Marlene, embodying all the worldly-wise sophistication of the war-weary European, sneeringly tells the Congresswoman what silly shrews American women are. Lund takes full advantage of his part as the de-Nazification officer whose biological urges triumph over duty, and Wilder affords Miss Dietrich eye-stealing, scene-stealing moments by making her a nightclub entertainer working in a cellar called The Lorelei.

The background was shot in Berlin by Wilder and Charles Lang, and *A Foreign Affair* came close to offering all things for all customers as a buoyant, refreshing diversion on the serious question of occupation of vanquished countries.

Sunset Boulevard is the second longest thoroughfare of Los Angeles—a street with more forms of human life than any pavement in America. It starts at Union Station downtown, where el Pueblo de la Reina de Los Angeles was born on top of an Indian village. As in most cities, life around the terminal is transient —small stores and people without families, neighbourhoods euphemistically called 'older sections'. The Boulevard straggles north-west a while through a sort of Hollywood has-been, then heads straight west through a motel lane and radio and television studios real estate until it becomes The Strip—a gaudy piece of neonland on the other side of the clock. When Los Angeles abruptly becomes Beverly Hills, Sunset becomes the boulevard of its film fame. Life is not visible; it goes on behind hedges and curving driveways—no stores, no offices, no petrol stations. It winds on past Bel Air, sprawling University of California, Los Angeles (UCLA), and keeps its dignity all the way to Pacific

Sunset Boulevard: two angles on a swimming-pool

Life with Norma Desmond: *Sunset Boulevard*

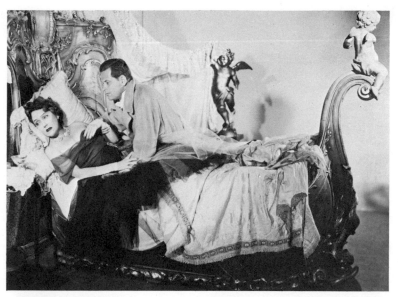

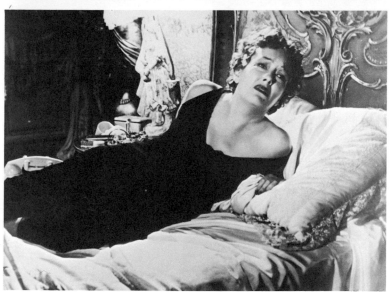

Palisades, curling the bottom of the canyons and ending at the ocean—an odd twenty miles from the railway beginning.

Sunset Boulevard moves both in time and space, passing besides the fabulous, historical Hollywood that F. Scott Fitzgerald was trying to write about in *The Last Tycoon* (one of the few Hollywood novels that isn't built on anger and self-pity), the mixture of fact and fiction Budd Schulberg poured into *What Makes Sammy Run* and *The Disenchanted*, and the shabby ludicrous landscapes of Nathanael West's *The Day of the Locust*: the Hollywood of vast fake Spanish Baroque. But the boulevard also touches the shores of the present-day hippie world, the Benzedrine dreamland and tomorrow's incubator set of sandalled girls, teen clubs and chaos. *Sunset Boulevard* is the best film ever made about Hollywood, a modern tragedy that has been called everything from a piece of dry ice to a pretentious slice of Roquefort.

Wilder's most famous film was not an overnight quickie. Brackett and Wilder had been working on an idea for a Hollywood-on-Hollywood story for two years. 'We had closed the doors and said: "What sort of a story shall we do?" ' says Brackett. 'Someone suggested a relationship between a silent-day queen and a young man; she living in the past, refusing to believe her days as a star are gone and holing up in one of those rundown, immense mansions. We saw the screenwriter as a nice guy, maybe from the Middle West, a man who can't make the grade in Hollywood and who is really down on his luck.'

Here the authors had got stuck, unable to figure out what should happen next, until one day when they were discussing Balzac's *Le Père Goriot*, one of them remarked: 'Suppose the old dame shoots the boy?'

Sunset Boulevard begins with a corpse floating in a Beverly Hills swimming-pool and the dead man's voice narrating the events of the few months preceding his death. Another, more macabre beginning was actually shot, a sequence that had the film start in the Los Angeles County Morgue in a long, narrow building with rows of metal slabs and on each a human figure covered by a

← Norma Desmond's final descent: *Sunset Boulevard*

sheet with only two bare feet showing. A Paramount news release of 22 August 1949, described the scene: 'Some three dozen extra players were called to portray corpses. They stretched out on the metal slabs which had been equipped with headrests to keep their heads from moving and, paradoxically, froze into immobility the moment Wilder called "Action!" ' At one end of the line, the corpse sat up and started to tell his story.

The characters in *Sunset Boulevard* are the faded psychotic silent-movie queen, Norma Desmond, played viciously without regard for sympathy by Gloria Swanson, and the younger writer Joe Gillis (William Holden) whom she traps. Both are washouts, flotsam on the back-shore of Hollywood, she a morbific and ageing movie idol, now forgotten and completely *passée*, and he a self-admitted failure who cannot write a worthwhile script. He makes one fruitless attempt to sell a bad script before succumbing to the humiliation of being her kept man, and later makes one last stab at writing a story with a young studio reader, a hopeful girl (Nancy Olson), but that, too, is doomed. Around them spins a fauna of rejects and has-beens; even the wholesome girl is the child of a family that *was* in the movies. Playing a one-man Greek chorus is Erich von Stroheim in the role of Max von Mayerling, Norma Desmond's butler-chauffeur, formerly her director-husband.

Cruel scenes abound. Norma's fortnightly bridge games with her old cronies, played by Anna Q. Nilsson, H. B. Warner and Buster Keaton, are classified by Joe as 'the waxworks'. To amuse her bored and pampered lover, Norma does her parasol-twisting take-off of a Mack Sennett bathing beauty and impersonates Charlie Chaplin. It is at this moment that Max chooses to let her know that Paramount is on the phone. The moustache and bowler-hat remain, but Chaplin vanishes; the Medusa mask comes back on her face and she says: 'Paramount. Ha! Let 'em wait. *I've* waited long enough!' Another much-quoted line is delivered with rare mastery: Gloria Swanson watching her young face in an old movie being shown in her private screening-room, and standing up into the murderous glare of the projector to cry, 'They don't make faces like that any more!'

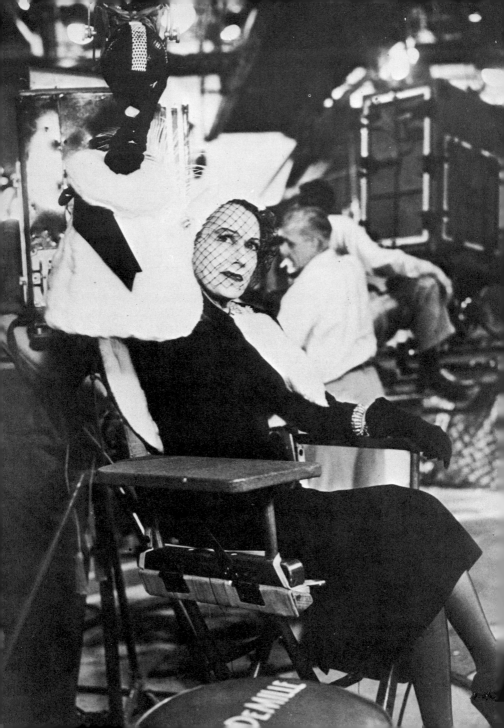

Wilder found Norma's mansion not on Sunset, but on Wilshire Boulevard, on the corner of Lorraine Avenue, where the Paul Getty family had an unused house (torn down in 1960). The house was a twenty-five-room French-Italian castle built in 1908 by a Mexican millionaire, and Wilder had the swimming-pool added as payment for using the premises. The glamorous, ship-shaped bed the movie queen sleeps in once belonged to Gaby Deslys, and her stately automobile was an Isotta-Fraschini which, new, had cost $30,000. The footage of herself which Norma watches was from the 1928 *Queen Kelly*, one of history's *films maudits*, directed by von Stroheim, and financed by and starring Gloria Swanson. Cecil B. DeMille, Wilder's confrère at Paramount, plays himself as the director telephoning her to ask whether he can rent the Isotta-Fraschini. Norma is persuaded that DeMille wants her, not the car, and no one dares tell her the truth.

The story grinds on until, inevitably, it ends in a head-on collision between illusion and reality, in violent death and staring madness. Feeling that her young lover is leaving her, Norma kills him. Then, faced by a barrage of reporters, police and newsreel cameras, she literally goes mad, and descends a staircase believing she's acting Salome in one of her movies.

Sunset Boulevard is a rare movie, full of exactness, cleverness, mastery and pleasure, a gnawing, haunting and ruthless film with a dank smell of corrosive delusion hanging over it. It was a worldwide success, with critics far removed from Hollywood seeing an exact self-portrait, and those closer to home applauding an etching of the fringe. *Newsweek* made *Sunset Boulevard* a cover story;* Georges Sadoul called it a grandiloquent study of Hollywood decrepitude;† François Chalais, reviewing it in the first issue of *Cahiers du Cinéma*, said it turned the inside out of the cinema. Bosley Crowther underlined that Wilder studiously kept the story on Hollywood's workday fringe and managed to 'tell nothing about the great nexus of filmmaking today,'‡ while James Agee said that

---

* *Newsweek*, 26 June 1950.
† *Histoire du Cinéma Mondial*, Flammarion, Paris.
‡ *New York Times*, 27 August 1950.

Silent star and sound microphone: Norma Desmond at Paramount by granting the silent era a kind of barbarous intensity, 'the contemporaries, by comparison, are small, smart, safe-playing, incapable of any kind of grandeur, good or bad',* which may add up to Wilder's toughest indictment of his Hollywood. Richard Griffith defended it against those claiming it was not a tragedy in an Aristotelian sense because it accomplished no purgation by saying: 'There is classic precedent for another kind of tragedy, the tragedy of the heartless, led on to their doom by passions which are ungovernable because there is no will to govern them. The emotion induced by this kind of tragedy is horror. On that score, *Sunset Boulevard* certainly qualifies, as also in its "curtain". At film's end, Joe lies murdered; Norma is mad. Seneca would have liked it.' †

In a larger perspective, *Sunset Boulevard*, with which the Wilder-Brackett association ends, brought the American *film noir* to its paroxysm. Also in 1950, John Huston cut up a poor anti-hero in *The Asphalt Jungle*; Elia Kazan examined a raw-nerved underworld in *Panic in the Streets*; Joseph Losey probed the prejudice against poor Mexican-Americans in *The Lawless* (known as *The Dividing Line* in Britain); and Jules Dassin, exiled in London as one of the 'Unfriendly Ten', sketched the pestilence behind professional sport in *Night and the City*. In the even larger perspective of cinema history, *Sunset Boulevard* is a unique glance in the mirror.

---

* *Films in Review*, May–June 1950.
† *Saturday Review of Literature*, 19 August 1950.

6: Three Times Black

Double Indemnity is the odd one out during the Brackett years; *Ace in the Hole* is Wilder's first solo and the industry was shaking its head; and *Stalag 17* is one of Billy's favourites.

Double Indemnity is Wilder's first really ambitious picture, a story replete with suspense for which credit must in large measure be given to the direction. Wilder and Raymond Chandler had concocted what the Hays Office called 'a blueprint for murder', but in a curious nod to *mise en scène*, the Production Code Office cleared the final film as if it were not the story, but the way it is told that mattered.

James M. Cain's *Liberty* story, 'Double Indemnity', was apparently based on a sensational murder of the 1920s, and Wilder's film emphasises this similarity. In the Snyder-Gray murder of 1927, Albert Snyder was sash-weighted to death in his Queens Village, New York home by his wife, Ruth, and her lover, Judd Gray. Both the fictional and the real murders were for the slain men's insurance; both were committed by the murdered men's wives and their lovers.

Set in Los Angeles, Wilder's film revolves mainly round the characterisations of Fred MacMurray, Barbara Stanwyck and Edward G. Robinson—the first two as the lovers, and Robinson as an insurance claims agent who balks the pair's 'perfect crime' from becoming what they intended it to appear—accidental death from a moving train, for which there would have been a double indemnity.

87

Double Indemnity: the house, the supermarket, the railway tracks, the death cell →

Barbara Stanwyck plays the wife of a Los Feliz Boulevard oil-man, and when MacMurray, the insurance salesman Walter Neff, becomes her paramour, they sell the husband an accidental death policy. They then kill him and place the body on a railway track. Their plans go awry, however, when MacMurray learns that she has been using him as a dupe, and he shoots her dead. The story is told in flashback, with the opening having MacMurray confessing the entire set-up into a dictaphone for use by his colleague Robinson.

Chandler hated the film and talked with acerbity about the collaboration with Wilder. 'Working with Billy Wilder on *Double Indemnity* was an agonising experience and has probably shortened my life, but I learned from it about as much about screenwriting as I am capable of learning, which is not very much,' Chandler wrote in 1950 to his English publisher, Hamish Hamilton.* 'Like every writer, or almost every writer who goes to Hollywood, I was convinced in the beginning that there must be some discoverable method of working in pictures which would not be completely stultifying to whatever creative talent one might happen to possess. But like others before me, I discovered that this was a dream.'

Written with Chandler in seven weeks and shot in forty days in the fall of 1943, *Double Indemnity* is a director's picture, and whatever Chandler's objections, the author of the original novel, Cain, liked it. So did a specialist in the genre—Alfred Hitchcock. 'Since *Double Indemnity*, the two most important words in motion pictures are Billy Wilder,' he wired, kidding Wilder's own advertising campaign which said, '*Double Indemnity*—the two most important words since D. W. Griffith's *Broken Blossoms*.' And the film has scenes worthy of the Master. Example: the lovers have just put their victim's body on the railway track and are getting ready to leave the spot. The suspense is gripping, yet mounts still higher when they get into the car to drive away. Barbara Stanwyck steps on the starter and nothing happens. Cold panic on both faces. No words. Finally, MacMurray reaches over and turns on the ignition, which she had forgotten.

* *Raymond Chandler Speaking*, Houghton Mifflin Co., Boston, 1962.

For the Hays Office of 1944, Wilder committed double in-fraction. His film details the actual carrying out of a crime, and a crime of passion at that, and the murderer is an intelligent man. Daringly, Wilder starts in reverse, giving the plot tip-off in the beginning when MacMurray, speaking into a dictaphone, says, 'I have killed a man,' and then proceeds to tell how he did it.

MacMurray resisted the role for a long time, and Paramount vetoed it because they couldn't see him as anything but a sax-tooting good boy. When he signed with 20th Century-Fox, the studio gave in; it was his last as a Paramount property, so why not. 'I have always felt that surprise is not as effective as suspense,' Wilder told newsmen at the première. 'By identifying the criminals right off the bat—and identifying ourselves with them—we can concentrate on what follows—their efforts to escape, the net closing, closing. George Raft turned the role down flat and that's when we knew we had a good picture.'

It is possible to count on the fingers of one hand the films that have come from Hollywood with an utter disregard for box-office values or potentialities. There have been von Stroheim's *Greed*, John Ford's *The Informer*, John Huston's *The Treasure of Sierra Madre*, perhaps one or two more. *Ace in the Hole* gleefully dissects human beings at their worst. The film, a clever original carrying an occasional sharp sting of truth, leaves a bad taste in the mouth. Extravagantly overplayed by Kirk Douglas, it loses its guile at the end, wrenching Douglas out of character, dragging in some fortuitous violence to pay him for his sins, and lengthening the ending for a shabby theatrical effect. But *Ace in the Hole* is so forceful in its own brash, intense, insulting way that it remains a remarkable moment in cinema history—a commercial *film maudit*. As a statement against life, as destructive criticism, and as report-age done in a cold, observant style, it has rarely been matched in the history of commercial film-making.

Ace in the Hole is the story of Chuck Tatum (Kirk Douglas), a boozed-up reporter working in Albuquerque, New Mexico, until he can hit the big time again. His opportunity comes with the

Kirk Douglas and Jan Sterling: *Ace in the Hole*

92

discovery of a man trapped alive in a cave-in. Remembering the nation-wide sensation of the Floyd Collins case in 1925 (which may well have suggested the entire film to Wilder), Tatum prepares to build his scoop. By shoring-up the crumbling tunnels, rescue-parties might extricate the entombed Leo Minosa (Richard Benedict) in a matter of hours; but Tatum points out to the local sheriff how useful prolonged publicity could be in his forthcoming election campaign, and arranges that the rescue be effected through a lengthy drilling process instead. The news goes out. The sensation-seekers start to gather, personalities from radio, TV and wire services pour into the area, and Tatum is the hero of the hour. Before the rescuers can reach him, Leo is dead.

All this is told with the hard cynicism that marked *Double Indemnity* and *The Lost Weekend*. Wilder's principals move compulsively, driven by dirty motives. Leo's wife Lorraine (Jan Sterling) is about to run off after the cave-in, but Tatum urges her to stay, indicating the profits she could make selling refreshments to the hordes of sensation-hunters. She stays. Tatum wants her only for his story—the loyal wife praying for her husband's safety. He asks her to go to the near-by chapel so that he can get pictures for his paper. 'I don't pray,' she tells him. 'Kneeling bags my nylons.'

Resistance to *Ace in the Hole* was so great that Paramount had to change the name to *The Big Carnival*; but under any name it stood out sourly, and the sick joke around Marathon Street was that Wilder should change the name to 'Ass in the Wringer'. To get back the negative cost, the studio took to sending relays of persuasive Press agents around city desks to explain that the picture's spectacle of trashy 'yellow' journalism was not directed against the Fourth Estate as such. Nothing helped, and even Bosley Crowther was harsh, feeling compelled to tell his readers that no reporter could get away with such an arrogant crime. 'The responsible element would not permit such a thing, and thus Wilder has given us not only a grim and harrowing film, but he has also given us a distortion almost as vicious as the journalistic trickery.'*

* *New York Times.*

The film was a disaster.

Hollywood nodded its head wisely. As had been predicted, the break-up of the W & B team had proved what the wisecracks knew all along—Wilder had no heart and less taste. He was a compassionless cynic whose excess of contempt for humanity had only been controlled and toned down by the elegant and wise old Brackett.

Ace in the Hole was shown at the Venice Film Festival in 1951, and banned in Singapore for portraying a facet of American life 'that might be misunderstood'.

'Fourteen men attended the West Coast première of *Stalag 17* last night at Warner Brothers Beverly Hills Theater with more than a passing interest,' wrote Florabel Muir in her column.* 'They all have one thing in common: they have been prisoners of war; eleven served hitches behind barbed wire during World War II; three were released from camps in Korea last May.' The columnist attended the supper-party following the screening. 'It was interesting to sit around and listen to the ex-POWs cut up the picture. Some of them thought this was wrong or that was wrong. One said he had never heard of men dancing together, another that the movie was fine entertainment, but called attention to the fact that the German officer was wearing a wrong uniform; a third said he couldn't get the same kick out of the comedy as the whole thing brought back such unhappy memories and he still can't laugh at them.'

Wilder needed a winner after *Ace in the Hole* but went on unrepenting. 'We are a nation of hecklers, the most hardboiled, undisciplined people in the world,' he thundered in interviews. 'First, our heroes smack their girls' faces with grapefruit, then they kick their mothers in wheelchairs downstairs, and now they slap their lady loves with wet towels. How much farther can we go?'

Wilder went right on, and his adaptation of the Donald Bevan-Edmund Trzcinski Broadway hit is bold humour, with William Holden incarnating the hardboiled heckler that George Segal portrays in Bryan Forbes's *King Rat* fourteen years later.

* *Los Angeles Mirror*, 16 July 1953.

Stalag 17: Harvey Lembeck, Robert Strauss

Wilder uses a suspense approach to the melodrama, with plenty
of leavening by-play in the humour springing from the confine-
ment of young males. The plot-nub is the uncovering of an informer among the GIs interned in the prison camp (the real
Stalag 17 was located near Krems, Austria); until the time his
identity is revealed, the film is tense. Wilder lets the suspense
slacken at this point, permitting the informer to become an
obvious, shifty-eyed stereotype—a change out of keeping with the
previous mood. The climax has prime suspect Holden uncovering
the real traitor, who is thrown to the Nazi machine-guns to cover
the escape of Holden and Don Taylor.

Charlton Heston was supposed to have played Sefton, the
cynical character trying to make the best of his prison lot, but
Holden is good in the part—a good, snarling Sefton. Otto Preminger plays the Camp Kommandant with obvious relish, and

Robert Strauss and Harvey Lembeck repeat their stage performances as the dumb Stosh and his only slightly brighter pal Harry.
Peter Graves is the obvious traitor.

Wilder has a preference for *Stalag 17*, finding that it contains
many good things. 'There are five or six minutes, sometimes only
thirty seconds, that I like in my pictures. Along with *Sunset
Boulevard*, *Stalag 17* is one of my favourites, perhaps because
there were eight minutes that were any good.'

7: Democratic Love, One with Marilyn, the Lindbergh Tailspin and Lubitsch Revisited

Sabrina is Wilder's last film for Paramount—a good-bye present that brought in enough millions to make up for the previous excursions into the lower depths of *homo americanus*. A couple of short wandering years follow: *The Seven Year Itch* is made for 20th Century-Fox, *The Spirit of St. Louis* for Warner Brothers, and *Love in the Afternoon* for Allied Artists. *Witness for the Prosecution* is made for United Artists, and with *Some Like It Hot*, Wilder settles with the Mirisch Company, releasing exclusively through United Artists.

Sabrina uses the Cinderella theme of Samuel Taylor's long-running Broadway comedy *Sabrina Fair*, and features one of its day's most incongruous screen duos—Audrey Hepburn and Humphrey Bogart. 'Gay as two grigs, they head the Oscar-studded cast in a picture with a high content of merriment, notably higher under Billy Wilder's directorship, than that of the original Broadway play,' said *Newsweek*.*

One cannot expect Wilder to be as sweet as Taylor, whose premise was that democracy ought to be a two-way street and that a chauffeur's daughter should be able to marry the son of her father's multi-millionaire employer. Wilder twists the plot, and in fact says that the chauffeur's daughter should be willing to accept the marriage proposal of either son of papa's employer. For the chauffeur's daughter (Audrey Hepburn) loves the younger playboy

* *Newsweek*, 30 August 1954.

Audrey Hepburn with Bogart and Holden in *Sabrina*

in the family (William Holden), and when the gold-lined scion begins to take notice of the orchid flowering in his father's garage, the elder brother (Bogart) moves in to break it up.

Sabrina is a Hollywood picture—wealthy characters, Long Island estate, Wall Street associations, Rolls Royce and Paris gowns. Wilder takes Taylor's play and spreads it out over the rich, luxurious area that was only suggested on the stage, thereby adding a great deal of atmosphere to it and endowing it with credibility. Slick quips abound, and Wilder gleefully lets his audience know the outcome long before his screen characters perceive it.

The shooting didn't go too well. Bogart characterised the film as 'a crock of crap', and is quoted by Ezra Goodman* as calling Wilder 'the kind of Prussian German with a riding-crop. He's the

---

* *The 50 Year Decline and Fall of Hollywood*, Simon & Schuster, New York, 1961.

type of director I don't like to work with. He works with the writer and excludes the actor. I didn't know what the end of the picture would be, as to who gets Sabrina. It irritated me so I went to work on him. I came in one morning and he gave me a two-page scene. I was not too impressed. "Billy," I said, "you got any kids?" "I have a daughter two years old," he said. "Did she write this?" I said. One thing led to another. . . .'

Wilder, granting that Bogart was 'a tremendously competent actor,' claimed the actor took tremendous joy in being a trouble-maker. 'Bogart would come to me and say, "Huston told me who he thought the ten greatest directors were and you were not on the list. Isn't that Huston a bum?" . . . But Bogart was a bore. You have to be much wittier to be mean, like Erich von Stroheim.'

The Seven Year Itch, which started shooting four months after the completion of *Sabrina*, is another Broadway adaptation. In George Axelrod's comedy about a shy husband's temporary bachelorhood, the emphasis was upon the husband, charmingly played by Tom Ewell, and the little chick upstairs was just the one real participant in his fancied extramarital career. She was a genuine and normal personality, and brought elements of sanity and wholesome candour to the lightweight little play.

In the film, carp-faced Ewell plays the summer bachelor, but the girl upstairs is fleshed out by the holy monster of the day—Marilyn Monroe—and this piece of glamour casting ruins the film. Marilyn Monroe is a fundamental man-trap, without wit and without discretion. 'When Miss Monroe turns up as a young lady too substantial for dreams, the picture is reduced to the level of a burlesque show, and Mr Ewell's efforts to be funny quietly are lost in the shuffle,' lectured the *New Yorker*.*

20th Century-Fox had told Marilyn Monroe that she would have to do *There's No Business Like Show Business* in order to get the lead in the comedy being prepared by Wilder, one of the few directors she had been told to trust. She had proved difficult during the shooting of *There's No Business Like Show Business*, complaining that Donald O'Connor, the male lead, looked younger

---

* *The New Yorker*, 11 June 1955.

than she and was three inches shorter, and she didn't trust her director, Walter Lang. She went through it, however, in order to work with Wilder, and shooting on *The Seven Year Itch* started as soon as the Walter Lang film was in the can.

Wilder went to New York for exteriors for *The Seven Year Itch*, but was less lucky with crowds than on *The Lost Weekend*. One scene called for Marilyn Monroe and Ewell to stroll along Lexington Avenue. It is a hot summer evening and they have just come out of a movie. To cool off, she stops on a subway grating while a train shoots by underneath, sending currents of air swirling up through the duct. The result is Marilyn's dress flying above her shoulders. The scene was shot at 2 a.m., when life is normally tranquil along Lexington Avenue. But somebody must have let out the news because 4,000 people turned up to see the Monroe skirt fly.

Marilyn was a good trouper during the shooting. She had started a twofold programme of self-improvement, undergoing psychoanalysis five times a week and taking private acting lessons with Paula Strasberg; but she was also breaking up with Joe DiMaggio and had started a religious kick. With Wilder, however, the big clashes were postponed until *Some Like It Hot*.

The Seven Year Itch was premièred 1 June 1955—Marilyn's birthday—at the Loew's State Theatre, jamming Broadway for blocks. It was a box-office success, and did more for Marilyn Monroe's career than it did for Wilder. She stayed with 20th Century-Fox, and on the strength of *The Seven Year Itch*, signed a contract giving her script and director approval. She had appeared in twenty-three films and had worked with twenty different directors. Of these, she found only three to be acceptable, and not one of these was one of the directors with whom she had made more than one picture. The three were Huston, Joseph Mankiewicz and Wilder.

Wilder left 20th Century-Fox, and for Warner Brothers made a $6 million flop. *The Spirit of St. Louis* was a filmed biography of Charles A. Lindbergh, with forty-seven-year-old James Stewart playing the sandy-haired twenty-five-year-old flyer who,

The Seven Year Itch: Marilyn Monroe and Tom Ewell with Robert Strauss (*top left*) and Sonny Tufts (*bottom left*) →

The Seven Year Itch: Marguerite Chapman and Tom Ewell

on 20 May 1927, climbed into the wicker seat of a twenty-seven-foot one-engined monoplane on a mud-soaked field on New York's Long Island and flew to Paris.

The historic Spirit of St. Louis now hangs in Washington's Smithsonian Institute. It cost $13,000 to build. The movie replica and its two stand-ins cost ten times that sum. For the historic take-off, Wilder built a 4,000-foot runway at the Santa Monica Airport. Then sequences were filmed in Long Island, downtown New York, and along the Great Circle flight-line—over Long Island Sound, Boston, Nova Scotia, Newfoundland, Dingle Bay in Ireland, down the Cornish coast past Land's End, across a choppy Channel, and on to the outskirts of Paris and a re-created Le Bourget.

The movie contains brilliant pieces of film-making, particularly the take-off from Roosevelt Field, where all the drama and tension of the memorable occasion are implied: Lindbergh shoving his five

The Spirit of St Louis

Love in the Afternoon →

Love in the Afternoon: Gary Cooper and Hepburn

ham-sandwiches into a pocket, his waving 'So long' to a handful of
bystandèrs, switching on the ignition, revving the 200-h.p. engine
and lifting his trembling little plane—loaded with 450 gallons of
fuel but no radio—up through a blanket of rain and fog, clearing
the telephone-poles by ten feet. Once in the air, Wilder suggests
with incisive and vivid images the fear and suspense as well as the
physical torture of the first one-man non-stop aeroplane flight
across the Atlantic.

To get away from the monotony of the thirty-three hours in the
cockpit, Wilder shows Lindbergh's early life in flashback fashion,
and it is here that the picture sags. The screen Lindbergh is as
stereo and pat as any Hollywood flying hero can be. Wilder shows
him flying through a storm as an Airmail pilot (the mail must get
through, is the message); he shows him buying a beat-up old
plane and setting about the task of raising money to buy a plane
for his transatlantic attempt—all this with the stubbornness and
resolution of an unmistakable James Stewart hero.

Love in the Afternoon: Audrey Hepburn and cello

Wilder appraised *The Spirit of St. Louis* with sparse candour. 'A bad decision. I succeeded a couple of moments, but I missed creating the character.' In his autobiography, Jack L. Warner confessed to his own puzzlement, 'The exhibitors are still moaning about it, and I have never been able to figure out why it flopped.'*

Love in the Afternoon is a dreamy love-story as balmy as a summer afternoon in Paris, in the tradition of witty and sophisticated Lubitsch screenfare. Even Gary Cooper in the role of an American Casanova is a re-enactment of the genre which first brought him fame—such blithe Lubitsch comedies as *Desire* with Marlene Dietrich, *Bluebeard's Eighth Wife* with Claudette Colbert, and *Design for Living* with Miriam Hopkins.

Cooper had wanted to do a film with Audrey Hepburn since he saw her in *Roman Holiday,* and things fell into place when Wilder

---

* *My First Hundred Years in Hollywood,* Random House, New York, 1964.

found Claude Anet's little book *Ariane*.* Writing together with I. A. L. Diamond for the first time, Wilder turned the book into an insubstantial soap-bubble glinting with humour and romance. 'I had a chance of getting Audrey Hepburn and I thought the picture could be good, with feelings, humour and everything,' he told a Paris news conference when shooting started at the Studios de Boulogne. Trauner had built the most lavish sets ever on a French sound-stage, including a full-scale replica of the second floor of the Ritz Hotel with corridors and working elevators, the entire first floor of the Paris Conservatoire, and a luxury suite.

As the cello-playing music student, Audrey Hepburn was required to learn the finger-movements for the cello part of Haydn's Eighty-eighth Symphony. One of the more spectacular scenes took place in the Opéra, where Wilder had 960 extras in evening gowns and white tie and tails fill the orchestra and boxes for a gala performance of *Tristan and Isolde*. Wilder paid tribute to a favourite song of his Viennese student days, 'Fascination', by making the haunting waltz serve as the background theme melody for the love scenes between Ariane Chevasse and Frank Flannagan. Bad weather marred exterior shooting and drove the cost up, particularly a picnic on a lake scene shot at Château de Vitry, forty miles from Paris.

Love in the Afternoon, with its Wilderian double-meaning title of romance between a very young girl and a mature man, has the flimsiest of plot-lines and the most sophisticated of *mises en scène*, complete with sensual and insinuating camera movements, soft focus for romantic compositions and sharp for the brighter comedy.

---

* By court order the *Love in the Afternoon* title in France.

8: Murder with Marlene and Slapstick with Marilyn

If *Love in the Afternoon* was shot in its natural habitat, *Witness for the Prosecution* was ground out on Stage 4 at Goldwyn Studios in an Old Bailey made by Trauner.

This short and friendly art director is a Hungarian, who never goes anywhere without his pet dachshund—a man who has a 'blueprint mind', as Wilder says, and who is a tireless worker of detail. Trauner's Old Bailey was his masterpiece to date. Spending days in London studying records and sketching the architecture (he was refused permission to photograph the courtroom), he spent another month figuring out and drawing ways to make the room more flexible for the camera. Although solidly built of Austrian oak, Trauner's $75,000 Old Bailey was collapsible and extendable. The sixty panels that enclosed the seat of justice were all removable, allowing filming from any angle, and the floor was made up of nineteen sections that could be added or removed as the director required.

Witness for the Prosecution reunited Wilder and Hornblow for the first time since *The Major and the Minor*, and Wilder and his old friend Marlene Dietrich for the first time since *A Foreign Affair*; but the brilliance in this Agatha Christie adaptation is courtroom suspense belonging to Charles Laughton. As the ailing barrister, he goes about his forensic duties with all the groaning, moaning, snorting, sniffling and drooling that the script can bear, and yet comes out like the sort of defence counsel anyone in the

Witness for the Prosecution: Laughton and Lanchester; Power and Dietrich

audience would want to retain if accused of giving a rich old lady her lethal lumps, as the story's hero (Tyrone Power) is. The mugging barrister sets the tone when he describes his reckless client as 'a drowning man clutching at a razor-blade.'

Wilder's direction, however, is responsible for the feat of keeping the rest of the cast credible. Power, as Leonard Vole, and Dietrich as his wife Christine, who startles everyone by turning witness for the Crown midway through her husband's trial, manage to be convincing through the various duplicities and mysteries that are never explained until Miss Christie rings down a series of curtains, each more ingenious than the last, clarifying everything and leaving the audience grinning idiotically for not having seen it all along.

Wilder wrote the screen version with Harry Kurnitz, a writer he called in again in 1967 to help polish up the last draft of *The Private Life of Sherlock Holmes*. He added several Wilderian touches, including a brawl scene showing how Vole met Christine in a Hamburg nightclub at the end of the Second World War. The scene employed 145 extras and 38 stuntmen, but when the battle smoke cleared, a noble mission had been accomplished—one leg, the left, of Miss Dietrich's trousers had been torn off. The plot-line has the sight of this leg—presumably a terrific box-office lure —convincing Vole that he loves its owner as he marries her on the spot.

This scene and a slow opening with some amiable by-play between the barrister and his peckish nurse (Elsa Lanchester) are unnecessary dalliances (possibly to bring the picture up to a commercial 116 minutes), but once they are out of the way, Wilder swiftly converts his Old Bailey into a tense arena of shifting loyalties and mounting suspicion, combining camera and script to keep the film from bogging down into tired courtroom clichés.

'You have to be orderly to shoot disorder; this was the best disorder we ever had,' Wilder told newsmen at the end of the shooting of *Some Like It Hot*. A typical Wilderism, the remark was more bitter than sweet because the filming of this slapstick comedy had been pure hell.

The film was produced under a complicated procedure designed to make everyone rich except the Internal Revenue Department. It was labelled an Ashton Production, presented by the Mirisch Company, and Marilyn Monroe didn't simply go to work for the producers—she became a partner in the venture. The corporate Marilyn Monroe Productions, Inc. had hardly gone to the Goldwyn Studios before the difficulties began. She went in for colour tests one day to learn that the picture would be in black and white. She did not want this at all. 'She had very strongly developed senses of self-preservation,' one of her biographers wrote;* 'she knew how she looked and how she was at her best—on a wide screen in full colour.' Wilder was concerned about the colour problem, not so much because of money as because of the nature of the film. 'In full colour Jack Lemmon and Tony Curtis would be accused of transvestism if their make-up was light, and of impossible vulgarism if it was heavy. Marilyn gave in, but not with very good grace.'

When the filming started, Marilyn Monroe was up to her old tricks. She was late; she was bad-tempered. She set the tone on the first day. The other actors had been on the set since 11 a.m., but knowing her proclivity for late arrival, Wilder had set her call for 1 p.m. She arrived at 3.30 p.m., swished into her dressing-room and shut the door. She didn't appear outside that door until after 6 p.m. Wilder dismissed the cast just before 6 p.m. and departed himself—which left her ready for action with no one to record it or play with.

The lesson didn't solve anything. She continued to be late, and muffed her lines, causing one set-up to go through fifty-nine takes. Wilder notes that in some of her multiple-take scenes, she got better and better, but her opposite actor often tired and played successively worse. This created fresh tensions and led to a blow-up with Tony Curtis. 'The question,' Wilder said, 'is whether

---

* Edwin P. Hoyt, *Marilyn, the Tragic Venus*, Duell, Sloan & Pearce, New York, 1965.

Some Like It Hot: the All-Girl orchestra

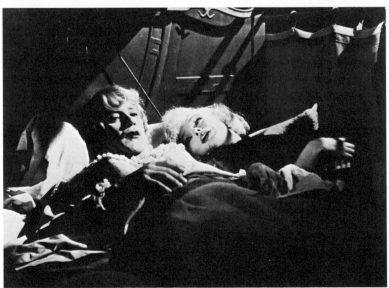

Some Like It Hot: Lemmon, Curtis and Marilyn

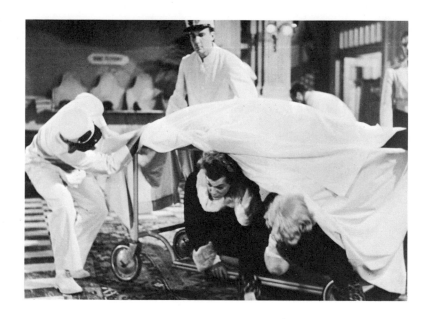

Marilyn is a person at all or one of the greatest DuPont products ever invented. She has breasts like granite; she defies gravity; and has a brain like Swiss cheese—full of holes. She hasn't the vaguest conception of the time of the day. She arrives late and tells you she couldn't find the studio and she's been working there for years. There are certain wonderful rascals in this world, like Monroe, and one day they lie down on an analyst's couch and out comes a clenched, dreary thing. It's better for Monroe not to be straightened out. The charm of her is her two left feet.'

At the end of the production, Wilder made other remarks in an unguarded moment and indicated he didn't want to work with her again. 'I have discussed this with my doctor and my psychiatrist and they tell me I'm too old and too rich to go through this again,' was one of his printable swipes. This brought a stiff demand for apology from Arthur Miller because, said Miller, Wilder had insulted his wife. Wilder tried to patch it up, but the break was not healed and his name was removed from MM's ever-shortening list of acceptable directors.*

Nevertheless, *Some Like It Hot* is a fast, racy and funny piece of nonsense in the best of the screwball traditions. Borrowing from every period of movie comedy, notably primitive slapstick and Marx Brothers zaniness, *Some Like It Hot* is madcap 1920s satire, depending for most of its humour on a sort of transvestite comedy carrying an ever-so-slender story-line, and Wilder thumbs his nose at just about every rule in the Hollywood book.

Lemmon and Curtis play a pair of seedy musicians—a saxophonist and a bass-player—who just happen to be in that garage when the St Valentine's Day Massacre of 1929 takes place. To avoid becoming the next victims of lawless Chicago, the two speakeasy dance-band musicians sign on with an all-girl orchestra *en route* to Florida. The singer with the band is Marilyn Monroe, known professionally as 'Sugar Kane', and the boys-as-girls in close quarters with real females aboard the train to Miami produce the expected fine crop of jokes. There is one scene in an upper berth of the sleeping-car that is the funniest thing of its kind since the Marx Brothers got trapped in that ship stateroom in *A Night at the Opera*. In Florida, Lemmon, in wig and skirts, catches the fancy of lascivious millionaire Joe E. Brown, while Curtis spends his spare time in men's clothing imitating Cary Grant to catch Marilyn.

To avoid the pitfalls of female impersonation, Wilder holds a tight rein on Lemmon and Curtis. To the audience, they are indisputably males, and the screenplay has them complain bitterly about having to wear feminine garb; and this constant carping is one of the things that keeps the masquerade from growing obnoxious. Wilder also quietly satirises some of the past films of George Raft, Pat O'Brien and Joe E. Brown: Raft, in spats, plays the gangland leader rubbing out a rival gang in the garage, and O'Brien is a Prohibition agent.

---

* Marilyn Monroe completed only two more films before her tragic death in 1962: *Let's Make Love* with George Cukor, and *The Misfits* with John Huston.

118

Some Like It Hot: the St Valentine's Day Massacre

Some Like It Hot was a success. It had grossed $14 million by 1962. It had cost nearly $3 million to film, and some said a million dollars of that cost was directly attributable to MM; but the profits were there, and Monroe earned $3 million herself.

9: A Rogue's Progress, Cold War and Rue Casanova

The Apartment is a dirty fairy-tale as only Billy Wilder can tell them. Its message is that a young man who lets his bosses use his furnished apartment to carry out extramarital affairs is operating in the best American tradition of individual initiative and enterprise. In this lusty story that can turn sad and ironic at any twist, Baxter (Jack Lemmon) is just another night-school diploma in the personnel files of a big insurance company in New York until the fateful day when it dawns on him that if his own virtues aren't enough, other people's vices might help. He lends his apartment to a department head who is having an affair with a telephone-operator. Soon he is slipping his key to four philandering executives, and though he gets awfully tired of sitting in the park all evening, keymanship has its compensations. His superiors write glowing reports on his work, and the reports soon come to the attention of the big boss (Fred MacMurray). 'Baxter, as far as I'm concerned, you're executive material,' he says . . . because he wants the key too. Before long, Baxter is an assistant to the boss. Suddenly he discovers that he has outsmarted himself—the girl that the boss takes to his apartment (Shirley MacLaine) is the girl of his dreams.

The Apartment is Wilder's best film since *Sunset Boulevard*, a bouncing comedy handling a frankly sordid theme with intelligence and compassion. The dialogue is frank; the picture has atmosphere; and it creates a feeling about people. There is a bit of

Jack Lemmon in *The Apartment*

The Apartment: Fred MacMurray (*above*), Ray Walston (*below*)

buffoonery in which bachelor Baxter uses a tennis racket as a spaghetti-strainer. There is a piece of business in which the heroine, when asked by him how many affairs she has had, admits to three but unconsciously lifts four fingers. There is a cruel vignette when she has tried to commit suicide and her top executive lover on the phone couldn't care less about her condition. There are unsavoury Wilderisms, such as the doctor's brutal treatment of the heroine after her suicide attempt; and there is Wilderian humour—the very premise that the rise of an organisation man is a sort of rogue's progress and that the room at the top is the executive washroom. Even the resolution is essential Wilder: Baxter turns in his washroom key and wins the girl. They will be happy, but jobless.

The filming of *The Apartment* at Goldwyn Studios was pleasant, relaxed, and Wilder was in top form, cracking jokes at every turn. He called the dolly shot at the beginning of the film, which takes Baxter through acres of grey steel desks and steel-grey faces on his first promotion, 'our chariot race'. The scene of the office Christmas party was actually shot on 23 December 1959. A notation in the script called it 'a swinging party', and Wilder's principals and 250 extras were on top at the first take. Beamed he: 'Who needs a director? I just say "Action!" and stand back.'

Wilder's constant obsession with pace in screen comedy found its own answer in *One, Two, Three*—a rapid, brutal and over-wrought comic statement on the Cold War. How fast is fast in comedy, Wilder asked himself. Can you machine-gun audiences with soundtrack satire? Do audiences have the stamina to pay close attention continuously, or must they come up for breath now and then? In London for the British première of *One, Two, Three*, he remarked that the tendency in contemporary films is length and slowness: 'I think because the critics think highly of European directors like Antonioni who have gotten away with it—the idea that slowness and solemnity are the same thing as profundity.' But he wondered if in *One, Two, Three* he hadn't gone too far with his 'experiment in keeping up the tempo the whole time.'

The Apartment: the office party

The plot of *One, Two, Three* is borrowed from a one-act play by Ferenc Molnar, who would be astonished to think that any hero of his could turn up as the manager of a Coca-Cola bottling plant. Yet that is what the picture's hero is. 'It is a farce that intentionally mocks and reverses every conventional attitude we have, or think we ought to have; virtue is punished, corruption and stupidity are rewarded and the whole German people, as if in a trifling aside, are indicted as lickspittles or martinets, and we sit watching and roaring with delight,' is the way Brendan Gill described the film. 'For this *tour de force* of fratricidal subversion, we have to thank not only Mr Cagney who makes it shamefully attractive, but, again, Mr Wilder, who produced and directed the picture and who could, no doubt, wring a hearty yock from bubonic plague.'* Reflecting on Wilder's ability to make bubonic plague into comedy, Pauline Kael felt that, except perhaps in a different way

* *The New Yorker*, 6 January 1962.

Cagney in *One, Two, Three*

in *Ace in the Hole*, Wilder had 'never before exhibited such a brazen contempt for people.'*

One, Two, Three—termed 'Hellzapoppin in Berlin' by some critics—is a coarsened remake of *Ninotchka*, with Horst Buchholz playing a Greta Garbo Communist in reverse, and Americans, Russians and Germans competing in petty corruption and shoddy sentimentality.

Wilder's direction is sharp and so furious that the *Variety* reviewer wondered if even the cream of an audience would catch more than seventy-five per cent of the significance of the dialogue at first hearing.† Cagney, who suffered from acute homesickness during the shooting in Germany, proves himself a good, snappy farceur with a glib, full-throttled characterisation. The staccato delivery wasn't always easy to film, and one speech during a shoe-shine session required fifty-two takes—only seven short of the all-time record with Marilyn Monroe on *Some Like It Hot*. While Buchholz and Pamela Tiffin fail to register much, Arlene Francis is just right as Mrs MacNamara, and some of the supporting roles are brutally in focus—Howard St John as the tycoon of Coca Colonisation, and Hanns Lothar as a heel-clicking right-hand man. Trauner's art direction contributes importantly to the comedy, notably in a scene set in a smoky East Berlin nightspot, and Andre Previn incorporates period pop themes like 'Yes, We Have no Bananas' with incongruous effect into his score.

One, Two, Three was shot in Berlin during the autumn of 1961 at a time when the East–West climate deteriorated daily, and before Wilder could yell 'Cut!' the last time, the Berlin Wall was under construction. Permission to shoot in East Berlin was revoked three weeks into production, forcing Wilder to have Trauner build a full-sized replica of the East side of the Brandenburg Gate on the back-lot of the Bavaria Studios in Munich.

Wilder managed one little revenge. He made a dry run of a shot up to the boundary-line, and then sent word to the heavily armed East German police that they were in the picture, and while it

---

* *I Lost it at the Movies*, Little, Brown & Co., Boston, 1965.
† *Variety*, 29 November 1961.

was all right with him, he was afraid it would give audiences the impression that East Berlin was a Police State. That cleared the gate for several hours.

Berlin fêted the former hanger-on from the Romanisches Café, declaring 1 July 1961 'Billy Wilder Day', and the wisecracking director had a field-day—grabbing headlines as fast as he could wring gags out of the mounting political crisis. At an East Berlin Press Conference at the start of the picture, East German officials said they would like to buy *The Apartment*, a criticism of capitalism that could only happen in New York. 'That's right, it could never happen in Moscow,' retorted Wilder. 'Nobody in Moscow has an apartment he can spare.'

And Coca-Cola? In interviews, Wilder admitted that the soft-drink company would get a lot of publicity, but that its public relations department viewed the portrayal of the firm's bosses as complete idiots with disfavour. He also claimed he had no tie-in with the Coke people but was keeping a promise made five years earlier when Gary Cooper played a Pepsi-Cola salesman in *Love in the Afternoon*. But who was he kidding? Coca-Cola provided truck banners, supermarket ads and window displays promoting *One, Two, Three* throughout the publicity campaign.

Elizabeth Taylor was more or less set for Wilder's next comedy, *Irma la Douce*, and Charles Laughton had been signed for the role of the philosophising *bistro*-owner, Moustache. Laughton died, and the part was scaled down from a *La Ronde*-type master of ceremonies and commentator role to the part actually played by Lou Jacobi, the café-proprietor always ending his stories with 'but that's another story.' Work on *The Apartment* with Jack Lemmon and Shirley MacLaine had been so pleasant that Wilder decided not to get in on the smouldering Liz Taylor-Richard Burton act (Joseph Mankiewicz was editing *Cleopatra* with Darryl Zanuck breathing down his neck at 20th Century-Fox while Wilder started *Irma la Douce* at the Goldwyn Studios).

In adapting Alexandre Breffort's musical, Iz Diamond and Wilder first removed the sixteen musical numbers, a daring piece

127

Jack Lemmon and Shirley MacLaine in *Irma la Douce*

of open-heart surgery that amputated their source-material of part of its identity and its stage charm, but also eliminated its conscious theatricality. Next, Wilder had his performers deliver the romantic comedy straight, relying on comic invention to do the service of music and dance.

Despite its setting in the Parisian *milieu*, Wilder's *Irma la Douce* is a moral morality play. Taking the brash tale of a prostitute and her pimp, Wilder turned it into a gay and stylish nothing-really-happens Feydeau imitation. He lets the audience know beyond question that the lady's profession is the world's oldest, and gives some humorous demonstrations of how she and her sisters ply their trade in Rue Casanova, but once Nestor (Lemmon) has fallen in love with Irma and she has made him her *mec*,* things change. To

* One of Wilder's snazzier in-jokes comes when the pimps form a union called 'The Mecs of Paris Protective Association', soon abbreviated to MPPA—the real-life acronym for Motion Picture Producers Association.

131

keep her to himself, Nestor disguises himself as a buck-toothed English peer who says he lost his manhood when the Bridge on the River Kwai fell on him . . . but who will pay a lot of francs to spend one night a week with her to play cards. These francs Nestor must earn toiling at the near-by Halles Market while Irma sleeps.

Lemmon and MacLaine aren't very French—which didn't prevent *Cahiers du Cinéma* from congratulating Wilder on having caught the quintessence of Gallic atmosphere and giving a nod to Trauner's re-creation of Paris. 'Nothing is missing—not a label, not an ashtray, not a door-knob, and this quasi-Viscontian attention to detail would be sufficient to move us; but the essence is elsewhere: in the way of coming to grips, beyond the liberties that fantasy allows, with atmosphere,' wrote Michel Mardore.* 'And, after all, why shy away from what is common? Hasn't Wilder been taken to task enough for his "vulgarity"? In his hymn to the "Paris Stomach" [as the Halles wholesale produce market is called] which opens *Irma la Douce*, it's easy to see Wilder's declaration of intent—which adds up to this: "I'm accused of being vulgar. So much the better. That proves I'm close to life." After all, real elegance makes mockery of good taste.'

Lemmon is little short of brilliant in several scenes, and Jean-Luc Godard was moved to call the acting of the Lemmon-MacLaine duo 'transparent', and Wilder's Panavision camera full of 'finesse and intensity'.† Despite its huge box-office success ($18 million by 1965), *Irma la Douce* is not one of Wilder's best, but a one-tracked and over-long exercise in Feydeau naughtiness. 'Mr Wilder worked harder than was needed with the readily available *Irma la Douce*,' summed up Bosley Crowther.‡

---

* *Cahiers du Cinéma* 149, November 1963.

† *Cahiers du Cinéma* 150–151, December 1963/January 1964 ('Dictionnaire de 121 metteurs en scène').

‡ *New York Times*, 6 June 1963.

10: Spooner, Gingrich and Holmes

'Peculiarly enough, the theme of *Kiss Me, Stupid* was human dignity and the sanctity of marriage,' said Wilder a year after the film had stirred up a furore of a magnitude that neither he nor anyone around him had expected. In 1965, this story of adultery and its rewards somehow was too stiff for the American opinion-makers. While the London *Times* exclaimed 'in a world all too obsessively infected with the cult of ghastly good taste, thank heaven for Mr Billy Wilder,' American public opinion boiled over with indignation. The film was slashed by critics and by the Catholic Church with such vehemence that even United Artists got jittery and talked Wilder into reshooting a couple of scenes.

Less than two years later, movies as 'dirty' or dirtier than *Kiss Me, Stupid* were, if not standard Hollywood fare, at least an element of most 'adult' screenfare. But in 1965, they let Wilder have it.

What he tells in *Kiss Me, Stupid* is an ironic tale of a one-night exchange of partners, a cuckolded husband who is none the wiser, and three others who are none the worse off for it all. Set in a fictitious desert town, the plot brings to life a squalid foursome—Ray Walston, the jealous husband, a piano-teacher and frustrated composer named Orville J. Spooner; Felicia Farr, his pretty, empty-headed wife, Zelda; Dean Martin, called Dino, who is a lecher and a singer in that order; and Kim Novak, a bar-girl or village whore called Polly the Pistol. When Dino, driving from

Kim Novak, Dean Martin and Ray Walston in *Kiss Me, Stupid* →

Las Vegas to Los Angeles, is detoured to Climax, Nevada, song-writer Spooner and his petrol station lyricist conspire to keep him in their town so they can make him listen to their songs. But Dino has a notorious reputation with women, and Spooner is afraid he will draw a bed with his wife. Spooner's solution to the problem is to hire—as a substitute for the evening—Polly the Pistol. Dino, it seems, gets terrible headaches unless he has a woman every night.

When Dino sets out to seduce the substitute, Spooner becomes jealous in spite of himself and throws the singer out of the house. Dino drives to a roadhouse and, of course, meets up with Zelda, who by now is sloppy drunk. He seduces her, or is seduced by her, and the next morning leaves $500 for her services. He also buys one of Spooner's songs. Spooner, in the meantime, has enjoyed a night with Polly. When Spooner hears one of his songs on nation-wide TV days later, he can't understand what happened. Zelda smiles, and at the fade-out says: 'Kiss Me, Stupid.'

The film received the quasi-automatic MPPA Production Code Seal, but the Catholic Church Legion of Decency objected. Exasperated by a long line of increasingly trashy films, such as *The Carpetbaggers*, *A House is not a Home* and *Where Love Has Gone*, which had fantastic successes at the box-office, the Legion decided to set an example of its still considerable power. But pre-view audiences had already told the United Artists people that they had a problem—and, in an unprecedented move, Wilder called back Dean Martin and Felicia Farr for a retake of the seduction.

In the new version, Martin apparently falls asleep, although the viewer is left to wonder whether he slept *all* night. It was this slightly cleaned-up version that was sent to the Legion for its rating. Rev. Mgr. Thomas F. Little gave *Kiss Me, Stupid* a C (Condemned) rating, and—again unprecedented—issued a wrathful blast at Wilder and his industry and advised America's forty million Catholics to stay away. His rating appendage said that Wilder 'has regrettably produced a thoroughly sordid piece of realism which is esthetically as well as morally repulsive. Crude and suggestive dialogue, a leering treatment of marital and extra-

← Felicia Farr in *Kiss Me, Stupid*

marital sex, prurient preoccupation with lechery compound the film's condonation of immorality.' One immediate result was that United Artists made a show of announcing that it would not release *Kiss Me, Stupid*. Then it quietly turned the film over to its subsidiary, Lopert Pictures, for U.S. distribution.

Wilder was dumbfounded. Some of the Legion's objections had amazed him, he told a New York news conference. 'Zelda Spooner is the kind of woman who makes her own preserves, sews her own clothes, grows her own parsley. When Dean Martin tries to shake Ray Walston, he tells Walston to make twelve copies of a song while he and "the wife" go out in the garden. "She can show me her parsley." The Legion objected. What do they want? Broccoli? . . . What the critics call dirty in our pictures, they call lusty in foreign films.' As examples of the lusty imports, Wilder pointed to *Tom Jones*, *Never on Sunday* and *The Girl with Green Eyes*—all of them, in his view, lustier than *Kiss Me, Stupid*.

But *Kiss Me, Stupid* IS crass with a constant coarseness, heavily stressed by double entendres, running through the picture. Perhaps the original casting could have saved some of it. Ray Walston is not a sympathetic Spooner; he is harsh and ugly, mostly assuming a grim, bulldog look which is meant to express bewilderment but registers as unpleasantly truculent, and one cannot help wondering how the film would have looked if Peter Sellers had been able to play the composer. Three weeks shooting of Sellers as Spooner had been completed when the actor suffered a near-fatal heart-attack; when it became apparent that he would be convalescing for six to nine months, Wilder was forced to replace him. Or a different Dino? Dean Martin is almost repellent in his leering. 'When this singularly dispassionate man makes a film without infallible charm stars, like Jack Lemmon or Marilyn Monroe, there is an appalled pursing of lips and wrinkling of noses, as though he had made a nasty mistake, like a puppy that isn't quite house-trained,' wrote J. H. Fenwick.* But over and above the plot's moral assumptions, *Kiss Me, Stupid* is a corrosive portrayal of backwater America, suffused with a despair that many

---

* *Sight and Sound*, Spring 1965.

The Fortune Cookie: Private-eye Purkey (Cliff Osmond); gold-digging wife (Judi West); victim, shyster and ferret-faced nurse (Maryesther Denver, Lemmon, Walter Matthau)

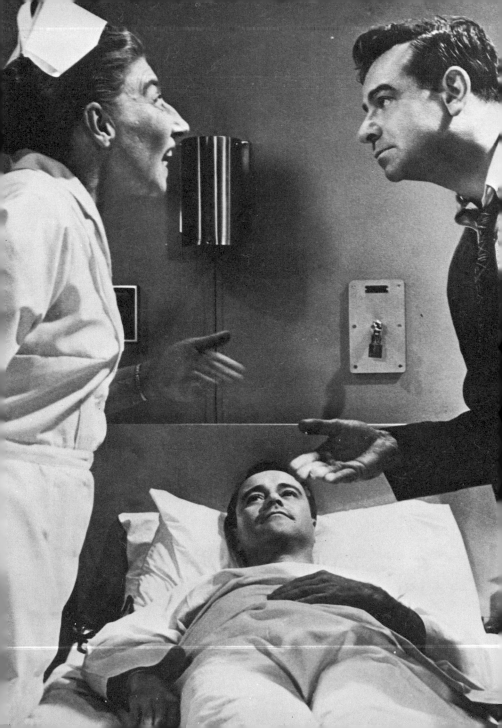

Americans prefer not to know. Climax, Nevada is a desolate place midway between Las Vegas and Los Angeles, and it has road signs to dream cities: Salt Lake, Reno. It is a town of fronts of frame-bungalows, where cocktail waitresses sleep in trailers surrounded by butane tanks, where time is told by television schedules, where no one is beautiful or gifted; a town where petrol-station attendants dream of hitting the big time—the gold record—a place where the flesh is urgent because nothing else is.

Wilder manages to make his characters touching at times—there is a very sad, funny scene where Zelda Spooner, getting drunk at the bar, vainly pleads with a jukebox to play her 'Melancholy Baby'—and to end his dirty joke with a happy ending of sorts. The composer gets his television plug for his songs, the waitress gets enough money to leave town, and the singer gets back to Hollywood without a headache.

'It's about greed, love, compassion, human understanding, but *not* about sex,' laughed Wilder as he started shooting *The Fortune Cookie*. 'Instead of f----, we have nuns in this one,' added Diamond, explaining that the film would have injured Jack Lemmon attended by sisters in a St Mark's hospital.

The Fortune Cookie, which became *Meet Whiplash Willie* in England, is about the gentle art of insurance fraud, very funny and very cruel; a wily morality play distinguished by the performances of Jack Lemmon and, even more, Walter Matthau, an actor little known outside New York theatre until this film. Lemmon is Harry Hinkle, a CBS-TV cameraman in Cleveland, who gets knocked unconscious in the course of covering a professional football game. When he wakes up in St Mark's Hospital, his shyster lawyer brother-in-law, Willie Gingrich, has already set things in motion. 'We're going for all the marbles, kid. You got a ringing in your ears and double vision. Your left leg is numb and you got no feeling in the first three fingers of your right hand. We're suing for a million bucks and we'll settle for a quarter million, tax free.'

Harry protests that he feels fine, but the brother-in-law convinces him that it will be best for everyone concerned if, for a change, he'd stop playing the good guy and just pretend. The film is Gingrich's twists and turns, plots and plans with the insurance companies, and the only thing that really stands between him and the successful carrying out of the fraud is Boom-Boom Jackson (Ron Rich), the Negro football-player who accidentally knocked the cameraman down.

The comedy is hard, clear and ruthless. Willie wheels and deals, the insurance companies put a pair of private investigators on the case, not at all convinced that Harry Hinkle needs his wheelchair, and Harry's renegade wife (Judi West) comes home as soon as she sniffs the musky scent of money. But Wilder sweetens his brew at the end. Harry regenerates himself at the last moment, just when riches are in his grasp, and manages to regenerate at the same time Boom-Boom Jackson, who has taken to drink to ease his stricken conscience. Willie Gingrich remains unrepentant, and is left figuring out how to sue his triumphant opponents for invasion of privacy; but the final scene is pure hallelujah—Harry and Boom-Boom tossing a ball and leaping about at night in an empty stadium.

'The pressures on Wilder to help maintain the American dream are probably immense,' said Hollis Alpert in his review of *The Fortune Cookie*.* 'Preston Sturges, too, you may remember, had to sweeten his brews, and with him gone, and Wilder playing it safe, satiric brilliance may be hard to locate in American movies for a while. From *Sunset Boulevard* to *Some Like It Hot*, Wilder was imaginative, raucous and had a way of running for touchdowns through a broken field of censors. This time around, he seems to have been tackled in advance.'

'The three greatest figures in fiction for the screen are Robinson Crusoe, Tarzan and Sherlock Holmes,' Wilder told Hedda Hopper in 1963. It wasn't until the fall of 1967 that Wilder could get *The Private Life of Sherlock Holmes* under way for a 1968 shooting start in London—later postponed to spring 1969.

'What we want to make is Holmes and Dr Watson when they

* *Saturday Review*, 24 September 1966.

were young, before they got famous,' said Wilder during the pre-production stage. 'Ours is the story of a friendship, so to speak, between two men.'

'The film will contain nothing of Conan Doyle, except the central characters and the Baker Street cadre,' said Wilder while shooting *Kiss Me, Stupid*. A year later, he nearly scrapped *The Private Life of Sherlock Holmes*, saying that the James Bond wave with its outlandish gadgetry would make a picture about the amateur detective in Baker Street look silly, if not downright ludicrous. He never said what changed his mind, but in the fall of 1967 he plunged into the project again with renewed energy.

II: Conclusion

'Well, nobody's perfect.'

last line in *Some Like It Hot*

After more than a quarter of a century in the arena, Billy Wilder means a kind of cinema that scrutinises things as they are, rather than how they should be—the cinema of a pragmatist and a moralist of sorts who thinks the flipside of medals can yield as much knowledge as the façade. The Wilderian camera is neither the sword of the reformer nor the sledgehammer of the incorruptible, but rather the Ariadne's thread that may help some of us feel a little better while groping our way out of the Labyrinth.

In the late 1960s, Wilder's *œuvre* is cast in what one may call a slightly anachronistic mould, but his films are contemporary because they deal with the here-and-now and because they are relevant when they are made. This preference for contemporary material explains why Wilder has never made a Western and only made two period pictures,* *The Emperor Waltz* and *The Spirit of St. Louis* (interestingly about his only two real fiascos). Movies age curiously, and it is not necessarily the ones couched deliberately in timelessness that stand out the crispest twenty-five years later.

Since his début as a director in 1941, following a good dozen years as a writer elbowing in from the fringe, Wilder has stood out as the Hollywood exception rather than the rule. Wilder and the cinema he makes, writes and directs are American and Hollywoodian, but within the 'system', both in its autocratic heyday

* Unless one counts *Some Like It Hot*, casually period but very contemporary.

and in its more tolerant contemporary form, the wily immigrant from Vienna has nearly always called the shots. From birth, the movies were hermaphrodite—half art and half lucre—but Wilder has always managed to have the upper hand on the moneymen without ever forgetting, of course, that in order to make another one, this one must be a winner. Though several Wilder films did fail to win, place or even show at the box-office, he has never had to make abject concessions to producers or audiences—a feat few big-time directors in any country can match over a twenty-five-year stretch.

Like Alfred Hitchcock, with whom he has in common that extraordinarily astute audience perception, Wilder may ultimately be making his films for himself, but he also *knows* that out there are a couple of million people willing to put down hard currency to follow his celluloid peregrinations. 'Madame Curie was nobody until people said "Hey, it works!" ' is the way Jerry Lewis describes this ill-defined *rapport* between creator (the film-creator in particular) and his vast invisible audience—the *rapport* that gives him confidence to blow millions of other people's dollars to explore yet newer avenues. Whether one calls this extra-sensory perception or good, old-fashioned Jewish common sense, Wilder understood very early this subtle two-way sensibility, and read the audience feedback loud and clear whether the message was 'It works!' or the opposite.

In the short history of film, Wilder is the screen's equivalent of Guy de Maupassant, an author of grand pessimism, sarcastic excess and sense for his time. Wilder's downcast point of view adds up to a human tableau that is both moral and cosmic, personal and traditional. His vision of the world can be both grandiose and shattering, but its ferocity too often reflects search for artistic effect, rather than expression of true anguish. And the limits of his talent lie here. Wilder creates films of a kind that force respect rather than affection. Too often, he will manipulate his audience and when the laughs threaten to dry up, throw in little sops of sentiment or go for the yocks with bubonic plague.

Enough has been said about his proverbial bad taste, and also about his origins in the Habsburg Vienna when it earned the title of 'gay' and launched a thousand musical comedies. His humour is Jewish and *saftig*, hard-sold and therapeutic—the little guy's self-defence against adversity and piled-up injustice and the big guy's safety-valve. Of film-makers, only Wilder could have planted in James Cagney's mouth, when Communists hijack his Coca-Cola, the line ' . . . and they don't even return the empties!' Only he could have made *Sunset Boulevard*, *Ace in the Hole* and, probably, *The Apartment*—highwire acts that break the rules with style, brilliance and corrosive thrills.

At their best, Wilder's movies sparkle with gross reality and risky propositions, cold wit and sardonic pathos. Now and then, among belly laughs or grins that don't know which way to turn, they say something serious and sad about the struggle for success. They often skirt disaster, and usually bring their points home with minimum pontification and maximum intelligence per square inch of film.

Will Wilder get yet wilder? Who knows . . . and why judge him with less generosity than he blows into his screen heroes? His future is *his*.

Meanwhile, on preview nights, he is busy convincing himself that his newest film isn't going to be the greatest—not the greatest hit, nor the greatest flop. 'Do they care, the audience in there— that's the important thing,' he said in Westwood the night *The Fortune Cookie* had its first tryout on a cold audience. 'Are they interested?'

Wilder was pacing outside, impatient with himself, with 'them', with the future. 'Do they care—that's the important thing. It's a brand-new game. I've invented the rules—do they want to play or not? Because they must do some work. It's just another picture, of course. It'll be on the bottom half of a double bill soon.'

Filmography

Billy Wilder
Born Vienna, Austria, 22 June 1906.
Educated at the Real Gymnasium and the University of Vienna (studying law). Went to France in 1933, America in 1934.

Films scripted but not directed by Wilder:
1929   *Menschen am Sonntag*/*People on Sunday* (director, Robert Siodmak).
1931   *Der Falsche Ehemann* (director, Johannes Guter; written with Paul Franck)
      Emil und die Detektive/*Emil and the Detectives* (director, Gerhard Lamprecht, from the novel by Erich Kästner)
      Ihre Hoheit Befiehlt (director, Hanns Schwarz; written with Paul Franck and Robert Liebmann)
      Der Mann, der Seinen Mörder Sucht (director, Robert Siodmak; written with Ludwig Hirschfeld and Kurt Siodmak, from the play by Ernst Neubach)
1932   *Das Blaue vom Himmel* (director, Viktor Janson; written with Max Kolpe)
      Ein Blonder Traum (director, Paul Martin; written with Walter Reisch)
      Es War Einmal Ein Walzer (director, Viktor Janson)
      Scampolo, ein Kind der Strasse (director, Hans Steinhoff; written with Max Kolpe, from the play by Dario Nicomedi)
1933   *Madame Wünscht Keine Kinder* (director, Hans Steinhoff; written with Max Kolpe, from the novel by Clément Vautel)
      Was Frauen Träumen (director, Geza von Bolvary; written with Franz Schulz)
1934   *Music in the Air* (director, Joe May; written with Howard I. Young)

148

1935   *Lottery Lover* (director, William Thiele; written with Franz Schulz)
1938   *Bluebeard's Eighth Wife* (director, Ernst Lubitsch; written with Charles Brackett
1939   *What a Life* (director, Jay Theodore Reed; written with Charles Brackett)
       Midnight (director, Mitchell Leisen; written with Charles Brackett)
       Ninotchka (director, Ernst Lubitsch; written with Charles Brackett and Walter Reisch)
1940   *Arise My Love* (director, Mitchell Leisen; written with Charles Brackett)
1941   *Hold Back the Dawn* (director, Mitchell Leisen; written with Charles Brackett)
       Ball of Fire (director, Howard Hawks; written with Charles Brackett, from a story by Wilder and Thomas Monroe)
1948   *A Song is Born* (director, Howard Hawks; a remake of *Ball of Fire*, written with Charles Brackett)

Films based on stories or ideas by Wilder:

1930   *Seitensprünge* (director, Stefan Szekely; written by Ludwig Biro, B. E. Lüthge and Karl Noti, from an idea by Wilder
1933   *Adorable* (director, William Dieterle; written by George Marion jun. and Jane Storm, based on a script by Wilder and Paul Franck) [An American remake of *Ihre Hoheit Befiehlt*, 1931, this film is incorrectly listed in most filmographies as a French film]
1934   *One Exciting Adventure* (director, Ernst L. Frank; written by William Hurlbut and Samuel Ornitz, from a story by Wilder and Franz Schulz)
1937   *Champagne Waltz* (director, A. Edward Sutherland; written by Don Hartman and Frank Butler, from a story by Wilder and H. S. Kraft)
1940   *Rhythm on the River* (director, Victor Schertzinger; written by Dwight Taylor, from a story by Wilder and Jacques Théry)

Mauvaise Graine (1933)

Production Company	Compagnie Nouvelle Commerciale
Producer	Général Édouard Corniglion-Molinier
Directors	Billy Wilder, Alexander Esway
Script	Alexander Esway, H. G. Lustig. Based on a story by Billy Wilder

Danielle Darrieux, Pierre Mingand, Raymond Galle, Paul Velsa, Jean Wall, Michel Duran, Maupi, Paul Escoffier.

Features

The Major and the Minor (1942)

Production Company	Paramount
Producer	Arthur Hornblow jun.
Director	Billy Wilder
Assistant Director	C. C. Coleman jun.
Script	Charles Brackett, Billy Wilder. Suggested by the play *Connie Goes Home* by Edward Childs Carpenter and the story *Sunny Goes Home* by Fannie Kilbourne
Director of Photography	Leo Tover
Editor	Doane Harrison
Art Directors	Hans Dreier, Roland Anderson
Music	Robert Emmett Dolan
Costumes	Edith Head
Sound Recordists	Harold Lewis, Don Johnson

Ginger Rogers (*Susan Applegate*), Ray Milland (*Major Kirby*), Rita Johnson (*Pamela Hill*), Robert Benchley (*Mr Osborne*), Diana Lynn (*Lucy Hill*), Edward Fielding (*Colonel Hill*), Frankie Thomas (*Cadet Osborne*), Raymond Roe (*Cadet Wigton*), Charles Smith (*Cadet Korner*), Larry Nunn (*Cadet Babcock*), Billy Dawson (*Cadet Miller*), Lela Rogers (*Mrs Applegate*), Aldrich Bowker (*Rev. Doyle*), Boyd Irwin (*Major Griscom*), Byron Shores (*Captain Durand*), Richard Fiske (*Will Duffy*), Norma Varden (*Mrs Osborne*), Gretl Dupont (*Mrs Shackleford*), Stanley Desmond, Billy Ray, Marie Blake, Mary Field.

Filmed at the Paramount Studio in Hollywood, March–May 1942. Tradeshown in U.S.A., 27 August 1942 (U.S. release date not available); first shown in G.B., December 1942. Running time, 100 mins. Distributors: Paramount (U.S.A. and G.B.).

Five Graves to Cairo (1943)

Production Company	Paramount
Producer	Charles Brackett
Director	Billy Wilder
Assistant Director	C. C. Coleman jun.
Script	Charles Brackett, Billy Wilder. Based on a play by Lajos Biro
Director of Photography	John F. Seitz
Editor	Doane Harrison
Art Directors	Hans Dreier, Ernst Fegte
Set Decorator	Bertram Granger
Music	Miklos Rozsa

| Costumes | Edith Head |
| Sound Recordists | Ferol Redd, Philip Wisdom |

Franchot Tone (*Bramble*), Anne Baxter (*Mouche*), Akim Tamiroff (*Farid*), Fortunio Bonanova (*General Sebastiano*), Peter Van Eyck (*Lieutenant Schwegler*), Erich von Stroheim (*Field-Marshal Erwin Rommel*), Konstantin Shayne (*Major von Buelow*), Fred Nurney (*Major Lamprecht*), Miles Mander (*Colonel Fitzhume*), Ian Keith (*Captain St Bride*).

Filmed on location at the Salton Sea, near Indio, California (a wildlife refuge at the southern end of the Mojave Desert), and in the desert outside Yuma, Arizona; also at the Paramount Studio in Hollywood, January–February 1943.
Tradeshown in U.S.A., 3 May 1943 (U.S. release date not available); first shown in G.B., 9 July 1943. Running time, 96 mins.
Distributors: Paramount (U.S.A. and G.B.).

Double Indemnity (1944)

Production Company	Paramount
Producer	Joseph Sistrom
Director	Billy Wilder
Assistant Director	C. C. Coleman jun.
Script	Billy Wilder, Raymond Chandler. Based on the story by James M. Cain
Director of Photography	John F. Seitz
Editor	Doane Harrison
Art Directors	Hans Dreier, Hal Pereira
Set Decorator	Bertram Granger
Music	Miklos Rozsa, with Symphony in D minor by César Franck
Sound	Stanley Cooley

Fred MacMurray (*Walter Neff*), Barbara Stanwyck (*Phyllis Dietrichson*), Edward G. Robinson (*Barton Keyes*), Porter Hall (*Mr Jackson*), Jean Heather (*Lola Dietrichson*), Tom Powers (*Mr Dietrichson*), Byron Barr (*Nino Zachette*), Richard Gaines (*Mr Norton*), Fortunio Bonanova (*Sam Gorlopis*), John Philliber (*Joe Pete*), Betty Farrington.

Filmed on location in Los Angeles and Hollywood, including Jerry's Market at Melrose Avenue in Hollywood; and at the Paramount Studio, September–November 1943.
Tradeshown in U.S.A., 21 April 1944 (U.S. release date not available); first shown in G.B., September 1944. Running time, 107 mins. (Twenty minutes were cut from the film after its first preview: the sequences cut were of Fred MacMurray's trial and his execution in the gas chamber.)
Distributors: Paramount (U.S.A. and G.B.).

The Lost Weekend (1945)

Production Company	Paramount
Producer	Charles Brackett
Director	Billy Wilder
Assistant Director	C. C. Coleman jun.
Script	Charles Brackett, Billy Wilder. Based on the novel by Charles R. Jackson
Director of Photography	John F. Seitz
Process Photography	Farciot Edouart
Special Photographic Effects	Gordon Jennings
Editor	Doane Harrison
Art Directors	Hans Dreier, Earl Hedrick
Set Decorator	Bertram Granger (supervisor on operatic sequence: Armando Agnini)
Music	Miklos Rozsa; also overture and opening aria of Verdi's *La Traviata*
Musical Director	Victor Young
Song 'Libiamo' from *La Traviata*	sung by John Garris and Theodora Lynch
Sound	Stanley Cooley
Medical Adviser	Dr George N. Thompson

Ray Milland (*Don Birnam*), Jane Wyman (*Helen St James*), Howard da Silva (*Nat*), Philip Terry (*Wick Birnam*), Doris Dowling (*Gloria*), Frank Faylen (*Bim*), Mary Young (*Mrs Deveridge*), Lillian Fontaine (*Mrs St James*), Anita Bolster (*Mrs Foley*), Lewis L. Russell (*Charles St James*), Helen Dickson (*Mrs Frink*), David Clyde (*Dave*), Eddie Laughton (*Mr Brophy*), Frank Orth, Clarence Muse; and Sophie (*Mrs Deveridge's Dog*).

Filmed on location in New York, in the Bellevue Hospital Alcoholic Ward, New York, and in Hollywood; and at the Paramount Studio in Hollywood, October–December 1944.
Released in U.S.A., 16 November 1945; G.B., 5 October 1945. Running time, 99 mins.
Distributors: Paramount (U.S.A. and G.B.).

The Emperor Waltz (1947)

Production Company	Paramount
Producer	Charles Brackett
Production Manager	Hugh Brown
Director	Billy Wilder
Assistant Director	C. C. Coleman jun.

Script	Charles Brackett, Billy Wilder
Script Supervisor	Ronald Lubin
Director of Photography	George Barnes
Colour Process	Technicolor
Process Photography	Farciot Edouart
Camera Operator	Lathrop Worth
Special Photographic Effects	Gordon Jennings
Editor	Doane Harrison
Art Directors	Hans Dreier, Franz Bachelin
Set Decorators	Sam Comer, Paul Huldschinsky
Music	Victor Young
Musical Associate	Troy Sanders
Vocal Arrangements	Joseph J. Lilley
Songs:	
'The Emperor Waltz'	Melody based on music by Johann Strauss, lyrics by Johnny Burke
'Friendly Mountains'	Melody based on Swiss airs, lyrics by Johnny Burke
'Get Yourself a Phonograph'	James Van Heusen and Johnny Burke
'A Kiss in Your Eyes'	Richard Heuberger and Johnny Burke
'I Kiss Your Hand, Madame'	Ralph Erwin and Fritz Rotter
'The Whistler and His Dog'	Arthur Pryor
Costumes	Edith Head, Gile Steele
Choreography	Billy Daniels
Sound	Stanley Cooley, John Cope

Bing Crosby (*Virgil Smith*), Joan Fontaine (*Johanna*), Roland Culver (*Baron Holenia*), Lucile Watson (*Princess Bitotska*), Richard Haydn (*Emperor Franz Josef*), Harold Vermilyea (*The Chancellor*), Sig Ruman (*Dr Semmelgries*), Bert Prival (*Chauffeur*), Alma Macrorie (*Proprietress of Tyrolean Inn*), Roberta Jonay (*Anita*), John Goldsworthy (*Obersthofmeister*), Gerald Mohr (*Marques Alonso*), Harry Allen (*Gamekeeper*), Paul De Corday (*Prince Istvan*), Julia Dean.

Filmed on location in Jasper National Park in the Canadian Rockies and at the Paramount Studio in Hollywood, June–September 1946.
Released in U.S.A., 2 July 1948; G.B., 30 April 1948. Running time, 106 mins.
Distributors: Paramount (U.S.A. and G.B.).

A Foreign Affair (1948)

Production Company	Paramount
Producer	Charles Brackett
Production Manager	Hugh Brown
Director	Billy Wilder
Assistant Director	C. C. Coleman jun.
Script	Charles Brackett, Billy Wilder, Richard L. Breen. Based on an original story by David Shaw
Script Supervisor	Harry Hogan
Adaptation	Robert Harari
Director of Photography	Charles B. Lang jun.
Process Photography	Farciot Edouart, Dewey Wrigley
Camera Operator	Guy Bennett
Special Photographic Effects	Gordon Jennings
Editor	Doane Harrison
Art Directors	Hans Dreier, Walter Tyler
Set Decorators	Sam Comer, Ross Dowd
Music	Frederick Hollander
Musical Director	Frederick Hollander
Songs: 'Black Market', 'Illusions', 'The Ruins of Berlin', 'Iowa Corn Song' and 'Meadowland'	Frederick Hollander; sung by Marlene Dietrich
Costumes	Edith Head
Sound	Hugo Grenzbach, Walter Oberst

Jean Arthur (*Phoebe Frost*), Marlene Dietrich (*Erika von Schluetow*), John Lund (*Captain John Pringle*), Millard Mitchell (*Colonel Rufus J. Plummer*), Bill Murphy (*Joe*), Stanley Prager (*Mike*), Peter von Zerneck (*Hans Otto Birgel*), Raymond Bond (*Pennecott*), Boyd Davis (*Griffin*), Robert Malcolm (*Kraus*), Charles Meredith (*Yandell*), Michael Raffeto (*Salvatore*), James Larmore (*Lieutenant Hornby*), Damian O'Flynn (*Lieutenant-Colonel*), Frank Fenton (*Major*), William Neff (*Lieutenant Lee Thompson*), Harland Tucker (*General McAndrew*), George Carleton (*General Finney*), Gordon Jones and Freddie Steele (*Military Police*).
Filmed on location in Berlin and at the Paramount Studio in Hollywood, December 1947–February 1948.
Released in U.S.A., 20 August 1948; G.B., 27 August 1948. Running time, 116 mins.
Distributors: Paramount (U.S.A. and G.B.).

Sunset Boulevard (1950)

Production Company	Paramount
Producer	Charles Brackett
Director	Billy Wilder
Assistant Director	C. C. Coleman jun.
Script	Charles Brackett, Billy Wilder, D. M. Marshman jun.
Director of Photography	John F. Seitz
Process Photography	Farciot Edouart
Special Photographic Effects	Gordon Jennings
Editorial Supervisor	Doane Harrison
Editor	Arthur Schmidt
Art Directors	Hans Dreier, John Meehan
Set Decorators	Sam Comer, Ray Moyer
Music	Franz Waxman; also 'Salome's Dance of the Seven Veils' by Richard Strauss
Song: 'The Paramount-Don't-Want-Me Blues'	Jay Livingston, Ray Evans
Sound	Harry Lindgren, John Cope

Gloria Swanson (*Norma Desmond*), William Holden (*Joe Gillis*), Erich von Stroheim (*Max von Mayerling*), Nancy Olson (*Betty Schaefer*), Fred Clark (*Sheldrake*), Jack Webb (*Artie Green*), Lloyd Gough (*Morino*), Cecil B. DeMille, Hedda Hopper, Buster Keaton, H. B. Warner, Ray Evans, Jay Livingston and Anna Q. Nilsson (*Themselves*), Franklyn Farnum (*Undertaker*), Larry Blake (*First Finance Man*), Charles Dayton (*Second Finance Man*), E. Mason Hopper, Virginia Randolph, Gertrude Astor, Eva Novak, Creighton Hale, Ralph Montgomery.

Filmed on location in Hollywood and in the Paramount Studio; and at the Paramount Studio in Hollywood, April–June 1949.
Released in U.S.A., August 1950; G.B., 17 August 1950. Running time, 111 mins.
Distributors: Paramount (U.S.A. and G.B.).

Ace in the Hole [also titled *The Big Carnival*] (1951)

Production Company	Paramount
Producer	Billy Wilder
Associate Producer	William Schorr
Director	Billy Wilder

Assistant Director	C. C. Coleman jun.
Script	Billy Wilder, Lesser Samuels, Walter Newman
Director of Photography	Charles Lang jun.
Pilot for Aerial Photography	Edwin Montgomery
Editors	Doane Harrison, Arthur Schmidt
Art Directors	Hal Pereira, Earl Hedrick
Music	Hugo Friedhofer
Song: 'We're Coming, Leo'	Ray Evans, Jay Livingston
Professional Advisers (journalists)	Agnes Underwood, Harold Hubbard, Wayne Scott, Dan Burroughs, Will Harrison
Sound	Harold Lewis, John Cope

Kirk Douglas (*Charles Tatum*), Jan Sterling (*Lorraine*), Bob Arthur (*Herbie Cook*), Porter Hall (*Jacob Q. Boot*), Frank Cady (*Mr Federber*), Richard Benedict (*Leo Minosa*), Ray Teal (*Sheriff*), Lewis Martin (*McCardle*), John Berkes (*Papa Minosa*), Frances Dominguez (*Mama Minosa*), Gene Evans (*Deputy Sheriff*), Frank Jaquet (*Smollett*), Harry Harvey (*Dr Hilton*), Bob Bumpas (*Radio Announcer*), Geraldine Hall (*Mrs Federber*), Richard Gaines (*Nagel*).

Filmed on location near Gallup, New Mexico, July–September 1950.
Released in U.S.A., July 1951; G.B., 15 June 1951. Running time, 111 mins.
Distributors: Paramount (U.S.A. and G.B.).

Stalag 17 (1953)

Production Company	Paramount
Producer	Billy Wilder
Associate Producer	William Schorr
Director	Billy Wilder
Assistant Director	C. C. Coleman jun.
Script	Billy Wilder, Edwin Blum. Based on the play by Donald Bevan and Edmund Trzcinski
Director of Photography	Ernest Laszlo
Special Photographic Effects	Gordon Jennings
Editorial Adviser	Doane Harrison
Editor	George Tomasini
Art Directors	Hal Pereira, Franz Bachelin
Music	Franz Waxman
Sound	Harold Lewis, Gene Garvin

William Holden (*Sefton*), Don Taylor (*Dunbar*), Robert Strauss (*Stosh*), Harvey Lembeck (*Harry*), Neville Brand (*Duke*), Richard Erdman (*Hoffy*), Otto Preminger (*Oberst Von Scherbach*), Peter Graves (*Price*), Gil Stratton jun. (*Cookie*), Jay Lawrence (*Bagradian*), Sig Ruman (*Schulz*), Michael Moore (*Manfredi*), Peter Baldwin (*Johnson*), Robinson Stone (*Joey*), Robert Shawley (*Blondie*), William Pierson (*Marko*), Edmund Trzcinski (*Triz*), Erwin Kalser, Herbert Street, Rodric Beckham, Jerry Gerber, William Mulcany, Russell Grower, Donald Cameron, James Dabney jun., Ralph Gaston.

Filmed on location in Calabassas, California, and at the Paramount Studio in Hollywood, February–March 1952.
Released in U.S.A., July 1953; G.B., 29 May 1953. Running time, 121 mins.
Distributors: Paramount (U.S.A. and G.B.).

Sabrina [British title: *Sabrina Fair*] (1954)

Production Company	Paramount
Producer	Billy Wilder
Director	Billy Wilder
Assistant Director	C. C. Coleman jun.
Script	Billy Wilder, Samuel Taylor, Ernest Lehman. Based on the play *Sabrina Fair* by Samuel Taylor
Director of Photography	Charles Lang jun.
Editorial Adviser	Doane Harrison
Editor	Arthur Schmidt
Art Directors	Hal Pereira, Walter Tyler
Set Decorators	Sam Comer, Ray Moyer
Music	Frederick Hollander
Songs:	
'Sabrina'	Wilson Stone
'Isn't It Romantic'	Richard Rodgers and Lorenz Hart
Sound	Harold Lewis, John Cope

Humphrey Bogart (*Linus Larrabee*), Audrey Hepburn (*Sabrina Fairchild*), William Holden (*David Larrabee*), John Williams (*Thomas Fairchild*), Walter Hampden (*Oliver Larrabee*), Martha Hyer (*Elizabeth Tyson*), Joan Vohs (*Gretchen van Horn*), Marcel Dalio (*Baron*), Marcel Hillaire (*The Professor*), Nella Walker (*Maude Larrabee*), Francis X. Bushman (*Mr Tyson*), Ellen Corby (*Miss McCardle*), Rand Harper.

Filmed on location on the Long Island Sound estate of Barney Balaban (President of Paramount Pictures), at Glen Cove, Long Island, and on Broadway, September–November 1953.

Released in U.S.A., October 1954; G.B., 9 September 1954. Running time, 114 mins.
Distributors: Paramount (U.S.A. and G.B.).

The Seven Year Itch (1955)

Production Company	20th Century-Fox. A Feldman Group Production
Producers	Charles K. Feldman, Billy Wilder
Associate Producer	Doane Harrison
Director	Billy Wilder
Assistant Director	Joseph E. Rickards
Script	Billy Wilder, George Axelrod. Based on the play by George Axelrod
Director of Photography	Milton Krasner (CinemaScope)
Colour Process	DeLuxe Colour
Colour Consultant	Leonard Doss
Special Photographic Effects	Ray Kellogg
Editor	Hugh S. Fowler
Art Directors	Lyle Wheeler, George W. Davis
Set Decorators	Walter M. Scott, Stuart A. Reiss
Music	Alfred Newman; Rachmaninoff's Piano Concerto No. 2
Title Design	Saul Bass
Sound	E. Clayton Ward, Harry M. Leonard

Marilyn Monroe (*The Girl*), Tom Ewell (*Richard Sherman*), Evelyn Keyes (*Helen Sherman*), Sonny Tufts (*Tom McKenzie*), Robert Strauss (*Kruhulik*), Oscar Homolka (*Dr Brubaker*), Marguerite Chapman (*Miss Morris*), Victor Moore (*Plumber*), Roxanne (*Elaine*), Donald MacBride (*Mr Brady*), Carolyn Jones (*Miss Finch*), Doro Merande (*Waitress*), Butch Bernard (*Ricky*), Dorothy Ford (*Girl*).

Filmed on location in New York and at the 20th Century-Fox Studios in Hollywood, September–November 1954.
Released in U.S.A., June 1955; G.B., 29 July 1955. Running time, 105 mins.
Distributors: 20th Century-Fox (U.S.A. and G.B.).

The Spirit of St. Louis (1957)

Production Company	Warner Brothers
Producer	Leland Hayward

Associate Producer	Doane Harrison
Production Consultant/ Montage	Charles Eames
Production Manager	Norman Cook
French Production Manager	Jean-Marie Loutrel
Director	Billy Wilder
Assistant Directors	Charles C. Coleman jun., Don Page
Script	Billy Wilder, Wendell Mayes. Based on the book by Charles A. Lindbergh
Adaptation	Charles Lederer
Directors of Photography	Robert Burks, J. Peverell Marley (Cinema-Scope)
Colour Process	WarnerColor
Camera Operator	Marc Fossard (in France only)
Technical Photographic Adviser	Ted McCord
Aerial Photography	Thomas Tutwiler
Aerial Supervisor	Paul Mantz
Editor	Arthur P. Schmidt
Art Director	Art Loel
Set Decorator	William L. Kuehl
Special Effects	H. F. Koenekamp, Louis Lichtenfield
Music/Musical Director	Franz Waxman
Orchestration	Leonid Raab
Sound	M. A. Merrick
Technical Advisers	Major-General Victor Bertrandias, U.S.A.F. (retired), Harlan A. Gurney

James Stewart (*Charles A. Lindbergh*), Murray Hamilton (*Bud Gurney*), Patricia Smith (*Mirror Girl*), Bartlett Robinson (*B. F. Mahoney*), Marc Connelly (*Father Hussman*), Arthur Space (*Donald Hall*), Charles Watts (*O. W. Schultz*), Robert Cornthwaite, David Orrick, Robert Burton, James Robertson jun., Maurice Manson, James O'Rear, Carleton Young, Harlan Warde, Dabs Greer, Paul Birch, David McMahon, Herb Lytton.

Filmed on location at Santa Monica Airport, Long Island, Manhattan, Guyancourt, near Versailles, and (aerial scenes) along the Great Circle flight-line, August 1955–March 1956.
Released in U.S.A., 20 April 1957; G.B., 23 May 1957. Running time, 135 mins.
Distributors: Warner Bros. (U.S.A. and G.B.).

Love in the Afternoon (1957)

Production Company	Allied Artists
Producer	Billy Wilder
Associate Producers	William Schorr, Doane Harrison
Director	Billy Wilder
Second Unit Director	Noel Howard
Assistant Director	Paul Feyder
Script	Billy Wilder, I. A. L. Diamond. Based on the novel *Ariane* by Claude Anet
Director of Photography	William Mellor
Editor	Leonid Azar
Art Director	Alexander Trauner
Musical Adaptation	Franz Waxman
Songs:	
'Fascination'	F. D. Marchetti and Maurice de Feraudy
'L'Ame des Poètes'	Charles Trenet
'C'est Si Bon'	Henri Betti and André Hornez
'Love in the Afternoon'	
'Ariane' and 'Hot Paprika'	Matty Malneck
Sound Editor	Del Harris
Sound	Jo De Bretagne

Gary Cooper (*Frank Flannagan*), Audrey Hepburn (*Ariane Chevasse*), Maurice Chevalier (*Claude Chevasse*), Van Doude (*Michel*), John McGiver (*Monsieur X*), Lise Bourdin (*Madame X*), Bonifas (*Commissioner of Police*), Audrey Wilder (*Brunette*), Gyula Kokas, Michel Kokas, George Cocos and Victor Gazzoli (*Four Gipsies*), Olga Valéry (*Lady with Dog*), Leila Croft and Valerie Croft (*Swedish Twins*), Charles Bouillard (*Valet at the Ritz*), Minerva Pious (*Maid at the Ritz*), Filo (*Flannagan's Chauffeur*), André Priez (*First Porter at the Ritz*), Gaidon (*Second Porter at the Ritz*), Gregory Gromoff (*Doorman at the Ritz*), Janine Dard and Claude Ariel (*Existentialists*), François Moustache (*Butcher*), Gloria France (*Client at Butcher's*), Jean Sylvain (*Baker*), Annie Roudier (*First Client at Baker's*), Jeanne Charblay (*Second Client at Baker's*), Odette Charblay (*Third Client at Baker's*), Gilbert Constant and Monique Saintey (*Lovers on Left Bank*), Jacques Préboist and Anne Laurent (*Lovers near the Seine*), Jacques Ary and Simone Vanlancker (*Lovers on Right Bank*), Richard Flagy (*Husband*), Jeanne Papir (*Wife*), Marcelle Broc (*First Rich Woman*), Marcelle Praince (*Second Rich Woman*), Guy Delorme (*Gigolo*), Olivia Chevalier (*Little Girl in the Gardens*), Solon Smith (*Little Boy in the Gardens*), Eve Marley and Jean Rieubon (*Tandemists*), Christian Lude, Charles Lemontier and Emile Mylos (*Generals*), Alexander Trauner

(*Artist*), Betty Schneider, Georges Perrault, Vera Boccadoro and Marc Aurian (*Couples under Water Wagon*), Bernard Musson (*Undertaker*), Michèle Selignac (*Widow*).

Filmed at the Studios de Boulogne and on location in suburban Paris, at the Opéra, and at the Château de Vitry, August–December 1956.
Released in U.S.A., 30 June 1957; G.B., 1 August 1957. Running time, 125 mins. (120 mins. in G.B.).
Distributors: United Artists (U.S.A.), Associated British Pathé (G.B.).

Witness for the Prosecution (1957)

Production Company	Theme Pictures. An Edward Small Presentation
Producer	Arthur Hornblow jun.
Production Manager	Ben Hersh
Director	Billy Wilder
Assistant Director	Emmett Emerson
Script	Billy Wilder, Harry Kurnitz. Based on the play and novel by Agatha Christie
Adaptation	Larry Marcus
Director of Photography	Russell Harlan
Editor	Daniel Mandell
Art Director	Alexander Trauner
Set Decorator	Howard Bristol
Music	Matty Malneck
Musical Director	Ernest Gold
Orchestration	Leonid Raab
Song: 'I Never Go There Any More'	Ralph Arthur Roberts and Jack Brooks
Sound	Fred Lau

Tyrone Power (*Leonard Vole*), Marlene Dietrich (*Christine Vole*), Charles Laughton (*Sir Wilfrid Robarts*), Elsa Lanchester (*Miss Plimsoll*), John Williams (*Brogan-Moore*), Henry Daniell (*Mayhew*), Ian Wolfe (*Carter*), Una O'Connor (*Janet McKenzie*), Torin Thatcher (*Mr Meyers*), Francis Compton (*Judge*), Norma Varden (*Mrs French*), Philip Tonge (*Inspector Hearne*), Ruta Lee (*Diana*), Molly Roden (*Miss McHugh*), Ottola Nesmith (*Miss Johnson*), Marjorie Eaton (*Miss O'Brien*).

Filmed at the Goldwyn Studios in Hollywood and on locations in England, June–August 1957.
Released in U.S.A., February 1958; G.B., 30 January 1958. Running time, 116 mins.
Distributors: United Artists (U.S.A. and G.B.).

Some Like It Hot (1959)

Production Company	An Ashton Picture. For the Mirisch Company
Producer	Billy Wilder
Associate Producers	Doane Harrison, I. A. L. Diamond
Director	Billy Wilder
Assistant Director	Sam Nelson
Script	Billy Wilder, I. A. L. Diamond. Suggested by an unpublished story by R. Thoeren and M. Logan
Director of Photography	Charles Lang jun.
Editor	Arthur Schmidt
Art Director	Ted Haworth
Set Decorator	Edward G. Boyle
Music	Adolph Deutsch
Song Supervisor	Matty Malneck
Songs:	
'Running Wild'	A. H. Gibbs and Leo Wood
'I Want to be Loved by You'	Herbert Stothart and Bert Kalmar
'I'm Through with Love'	Matty Malneck and Gus Kahn
Costumes	Marilyn Monroe's gowns by Orry Kelly
Sound	Fred Lau

Marilyn Monroe (*'Sugar Kane'*), Tony Curtis (*Joe*), Jack Lemmon (*Jerry*), George Raft (*Spats Colombo*), Pat O'Brien (*Mulligan*), Joe E. Brown (*Osgood Fielding*), Nehemiah Persoff (*Bonaparte*), Joan Shawlee (*Sue*), Billy Gray (*Poliakoff*), George E. Stone (*Toothpick*), Dave Barry (*Beinstock*), Mike Mazurki and Harry Wilson (*Spats's Henchmen*), Beverly Wills (*Dolores*), Barbara Drew (*Nellie*), Edward G. Robinson jun. (*Paradise*).

Filmed at the Goldwyn Studios in Hollywood and on location near San Diego, at the Coronado Beach Hotel and in downtown Los Angeles, August–November 1958.
Released in U.S.A., March 1959; G.B., 14 May 1959. Running time, 121 mins.
Distributors: United Artists (U.S.A. and G.B.).

The Apartment (1960)

Production Company	Mirisch Company
Producer	Billy Wilder
Associate Producers	Doane Harrison, I. A. L. Diamond

Production Manager	Allen K. Wood
Director	Billy Wilder
Assistant Director	Hal Polaire
Script	Billy Wilder, I. A. L. Diamond
Director of Photography	Joseph LaShelle (Panavision)
Editor	Daniel Mandell
Art Director	Alexander Trauner
Set Decorator	Edward G. Boyle
Special Effects	Milton Rice
Sound	Fred Lau

Jack Lemmon (*C. C. Baxter*), Shirley MacLaine (*Fran Kubelik*), Fred MacMurray (*J. D. Sheldrake*), Ray Walston (*Dobisch*), David Lewis (*Kirkeby*), Jack Kruschen (*Dr Dreyfuss*), Joan Shawlee (*Sylvia*), Edie Adams (*Miss Olsen*), Hope Holiday (*Margie MacDougall*), Johnny Seven (*Karl Matuschka*), Naomi Stevens (*Mrs Dreyfuss*), Frances Weintraub Lax (*Mrs Lieberman*), Joyce Jameson (*The Blonde*), Willard Waterman (*Vanderhof*), David White (*Eichelberger*), Benny Burt (*The Bartender*), Hal Smith (*The Santa Claus*).

Filmed on location in New York City and at the Goldwyn Studios in Hollywood, November 1959–February 1960.
Released in U.S.A., June 1960; G.B., 20 July 1960. Running time, 125 mins.
Distributors: United Artists (U.S.A. and G.B.).

One, Two, Three (1961)

Production Company	Mirisch/Pyramid
Producer	Billy Wilder
Associate Producers	I. A. L. Diamond, Doane Harrison
Production Managers	William Calihan, Werner Fischer
Director	Billy Wilder
Second Unit Director	André Smagghe
Assistant Director	Tom Pevsner
Script	Billy Wilder, I. A. L. Diamond. Based on the one-act play by Ferenc Molnar
Director of Photography	Daniel Fapp (Panavision)
Editor	Daniel Mandell
Art Director	Alexander Trauner
Special Effects	Milton Rice
Music	Andre Previn
Sound	Basil Fenton-Smith

James Cagney (*C. R. MacNamara*), Horst Buchholz (*Otto Ludwig Piffl*), Pamela Tiffin (*Scarlett*), Arlene Francis (*Mrs MacNamara*), Lilo Pulver (*Ingeborg*), Howard St John (*Hazeltine*), Hanns Lothar (*Schlemmer*), Leon Askin (*Peripetchikoff*), Peter Capell (*Mishkin*), Ralf Wolter (*Borodenko*), Karl Lieffen (*Fritz*), Henning Schluter (*Dr Bauer*), Hubert von Meyerinck (*Count von Droste-Schattenburg*), Lois Bolton (*Mrs Hazeltine*), Tile Kiwe (*Newspaperman*), Karl Ludwig Lindt (*Zeidlitz*), Red Buttons (*Military Police Sergeant*), John Allen (*Tommy MacNamara*), Christine Allen (*Cindy MacNamara*), Rose Renee Roth (*Bertha*), Ivan Arnold (*Military Police Corporal*), Helmud Schmid (*East German Police Corporal*), Otto Friebel (*East German Interrogator*), Werner Buttler (*East German Police Sergeant*), Klaus Becker (*Second Policeman*), Siegfried Dornbusch (*Third Policeman*), Paul Bos (*Krause*), Max Buschbaum (*Tailor*), Jaspar Von Oertzen (*Haberdasher*), Inga de Toro (*Stewardess*), Jacques Chevalier (*Pierre*), Werner Hassenland (*Shoeman*), Abi Von Hasse.

Filmed on location in West Berlin and at the Bavaria Studios in Munich, June–September 1961.
Released in U.S.A., December 1961; G.B., 8 February 1962. Running time, 115 mins.
Distributors: United Artists (U.S.A. and G.B.).

Irma la Douce (1963)

Production Company	Phalanx/Mirisch/Edward L. Alperson
Producer	Billy Wilder
Associate Producers	I. A. L. Diamond, Doane Harrison
Production Supervisor	Allen K. Wood
Director	Billy Wilder
Assistant Director	Hal Polaire
Script	Billy Wilder, I. A. L. Diamond. Based on the play by Alexandre Breffort
Director of Photography	Joseph LaShelle (Panavision)
Colour Process	Technicolor
Editor	Daniel Mandell
Art Director	Alexander Trauner
Set Decorators	Edward G. Boyle, Maurice Barnathan
Special Effects	Milton Rice
Music	Andre Previn (score for original stage musical by Marguerite Monnot)
Costumes	Orry Kelly
Sound	Robert Martin

Technical Advisers   Christian Ferry, Maurice Barnathan
Dog-Trainer   Pat La Cosa

Jack Lemmon (*Nestor*), Shirley MacLaine (*Irma la Douce*), Lou Jacobi
(*Moustache*), Bruce Yarnell (*Hippolyte*), Herschel Bernardi (Lefevre),
Hope Holiday (*Lolita*), Joan Shawlee (*Amazon Annie*), Grace Lee
Whitney (*Kiki the Cossack*), Tura Santana (*Suzette Wong*), Harriet
Young (*Mimi the Maumau*), Paul Dubov (*André*), Howard McNear
(*Concierge*), Cliff Osmond (*Police Sergeant*), Diki Lerner (*Jojo*), Herb
Jones (*Casablanca Charlie*), Ruth and Jane Earl (*Zebra Twins*), Lou
Krugman (*First Customer*), John Alvin (*Second Customer*), James Brown
(*Customer from Texas*), Bill Bixby (*Tattooed Sailor*), Susan Woods (*Poule
with Balcony*), Sheryl Deauville (*Carmen*), Billy Beck (*Officer Dupont*),
Jack Sahakian (*Jack*), Don Diamond (*Man with Samples*), Edgar Barrier
(*General Lafayette*), Richard Peel (*Englishman*), Joe Palma (*Prison Guard*).

Filmed at the Goldwyn Studios in Hollywood and on location in Paris,
October 1962–February 1963.
Released in U.S.A., July 1963; G.B., 13 February 1964. Running time,
147 mins (141 mins in G.B.).
Distributors: United Artists (U.S.A. and G.B.).

Kiss Me, Stupid (1964)

Production Company	Mirisch/Phalanx
Producer	Billy Wilder
Associate Producers	Doane Harrison, I. A. L. Diamond
Production Manager	Allen K. Wood
Director	Billy Wilder
Assistant Director	C. C. Coleman jun.
Script	Billy Wilder, I. A. L. Diamond. Suggested by the play *L'Ora Della Fantasia* by Anna Bonacci
Director of Photography	Joseph LaShelle (Panavision)
Editor	Daniel Mandell
Production Designer	Alexander Trauner
Art Director	Robert Luthardt
Set Decorator	Edward G. Boyle
Special Effects	Milton Rice
Music	Andre Previn
Songs: 'Sophia', 'I'm a Poached Egg' and 'All the Livelong Day'	George Gershwin and Ira Gershwin

| Choreography | Wally Green |
| Sound | Robert Martin |

Dean Martin (*Dino*), Kim Novak (*Polly the Pistol*), Ray Walston (*Orville J. Spooner*), Felicia Farr (*Zelda Spooner*), Cliff Osmond (*Barney Millsap*), Barbara Pepper (*Big Bertha*), Doro Merande (*Mrs Pettibone*), Howard McNear (*Mr Pettibone*), Henry Gibson (*Smith*), Alan Dexter (*Wesson*), Tommy Nolan (*Johnnie Mulligan*), Alice Pearce (*Mrs Mulligan*), John Fiedler (*Rev. Carruthers*), Arlen Stuart (*Rosalie Schultz*), Cliff Norton (*Mack Gray*), James Ward (*Milkman*), Mel Blanc (*Dr Sheldrake*), Bobo Lewis (*Waitress*), Bern Hoffman (*Bartender*), Susan Weddell (*First Showgirl*), Eileen O'Neill (*Second Showgirl*), Gene Darfler (*Nevada State Trooper*), Henry Beckman (*Truck Driver*), Laurie Fontaine, Mary Jane Saunders, Kathy Garber, Cliff Osmond; and Sam the Parakeet.

Filmed on the sound-stages of the Goldwyn Studios and on the back-lot of the Universal Studio in Hollywood, and on location in Las Vegas, March–July 1964.
Released in U.S.A., December 1964; G.B., 25 February 1965. Running time, 124 mins.
Distributors: Lopert Pictures (U.S.A.), United Artists (G.B.).

The Fortune Cookie [British title: *Meet Whiplash Willie*] (1966)

Production Company	Mirisch/Phalanx/Jalem
Producer	Billy Wilder
Associate Producers	I. A. L. Diamond, Doane Harrison
Production Supervisor	Allen K. Wood
Unit Manager	Patrick J. Palmer
Director	Billy Wilder
Assistant Director	Jack Reddish
Script	Billy Wilder, I. A. L. Diamond
Director of Photography	Joseph LaShelle (Panavision)
Editor	Daniel Mandell
Art Director	Robert Luthardt
Set Decorator	Edward G. Boyle
Special Effects	Sass Bedig
Music	Andre Previn
Sound	Robert Martin

Jack Lemmon (*Harry Hinkle*), Walter Matthau (*Willie Gingrich*), Ron Rich (*Boom-Boom Jackson*), Cliff Osmond (*Mr Purkey*), Judi West (*Sandy*), Lurene Tuttle (*Mother Hinkle*), Harry Holcombe (*O'Brien*), Les Tremayne (*Thompson*), Marge Redmond (*Charlotte Gingrich*), Noam

Pitlik (*Max*), Harry Davis (*Dr Krugman*), Ann Shoemaker (*Sister Veronica*), Maryesther Denver (*Ferret-faced Nurse*), Lauren Gilbert (*Kincaid*), Ned Glass (*Doc Schindler*), Sig Ruman (*Professor Winterhalter*), Archie Moore (*Mr Jackson*), Howard McNear (*Mr Cimoli*), Bill Christopher (*Intern*), Bartlett Robinson, Robert P. Lieb, Martin Blaine and Ben Wright (*The Specialists*), Dodie Heath (*Nun*), Herbie Faye (*Maury*), Judy Pace (*Elvira*), Billy Beck (*Locker-Room Attendant*), Helen Kleeb (*Receptionist*), Lisa Jill (*Ginger*), John Todd Roberts (*Jeffrey*), Keith Jackson (*Football Announcer*), Herb Ellis (*TV Director*), Don Reed (*Newscaster*), Louise Vienna (*Girl in Telecommercial*), Bob Dogin (*Man in Bar*).

Filmed on location in Cleveland, Ohio and at the Goldwyn Studios in Hollywood, October 1965–January 1966.
Released in U.S.A., November 1966; G.B., 18 May 1967. Running time, 126 mins (124 mins in G.B.).
Distributors: United Artists (U.S.A. and G.B.).

The Private Life of Sherlock Holmes (1969)

Production Company	Mirisch
Producer	Billy Wilder
Director	Billy Wilder
Script	Billy Wilder, I. A. L. Diamond

Robert Stephens (*Sherlock Holmes*), Richard Attenborough (*Dr Watson*).

To be filmed in England.

Acknowledgements

I wish to express my gratitude to The Academy of Motion Picture Arts and Sciences and its librarian, Mrs Helen Schwartz.
I wish to thank Mrs Stewart, Billy Wilder's longtime personal secretary, who has patiently corrected the manuscript; and Miss Sally Guye and Mr Yale Udoff for editorial advice.

A.M., Hollywood, November 1967

167

Wilder and Kim Novak on the set of *Kiss Me, Stupid* →